# CLOSING THE GAP

# Closing the Gap

## STEVE FLASHMAN

KINGSWAY PUBLICATIONS
EASTBOURNE

*Front cover photo (left): The Telegraph Colour Library*
*Front cover photo (right) and design by Drummond Chapman*

**British Library Cataloguing in Publication Data**

Flashman, Steve
    Closing the gap.
    1. Church work with youth—Great Britain
    I. Title
    259' .2' 0941      BV4447

    ISBN 0-86065-481-8

Printed in Great Britain for
KINGSWAY PUBLICATIONS LTD
Lottbridge Drove, Eastbourne, E. Sussex BN23 6NT by
Richard Clay Ltd, Bungay, Suffolk.
Typeset by Nuprint Ltd, Harpenden, Herts AL5 4SE

# Contents

# Introduction

This book is not meant to be a biography. There are many people who have led far more exciting lives than I have. Yet every life is packed full of learning situations and for this book to ring true and have an authenticity about it, it must be earthed in real life. So I have drawn freely on my own experiences to illustrate truths that are vital to grasp if we are to break through into the nineties with a new credibility and effectiveness, triggered by love for God and his world.

So let me give you a little information about my personal background to help set the scene for the things we will explore.

I had a tremendous amount of support from my parents who nurtured me in the things of God from childhood. They both had bad experiences with broken relationships in the past, but now God was cementing us together as a family and with my two brothers and sister, who all married when I was quite young, we have experienced a bond that is quite rare in family life today. It wasn't until I became an adult that I looked back and saw how God had been fitting the pieces together. My mother had knelt down by her bedside and given me over into the service of the Lord even before I was born. The simplicity, yet awesomeness of this act, made me realize the significance of a life in the eyes of a loving God.

I have never been very 'academic'. Sifting through old school reports is a humiliating exercise! I was born in Stepney, East London, but spent most of my childhood in South London. At Tulse Hill Comprehensive School my educational career peaked with comments from the teachers like: 'Good will, but possesses not enough capacity'; 'classwork rather slapdash'; and from a Mr D. J. Moon, the music teacher, 'He must find a little more self-confidence and then he should do very well.' I was later to encounter Derek Moon as a contemporary of mine at Spurgeon's College training for the Baptist ministry!

It was in my early teenage years that I began to see God at work in a way that I'd never seen before. My parents and I moved from London to the Isle of Sheppey in Kent. My parents started a youth club in their home and before long the place was packed every week with kids eager to hear more about God. We soon moved out to the local Baptist church, affectionately called 'The Tin Chapel', and saw this club grow rapidly until we had a group of around seventy every week.

I began to learn fast through a variety of experiences, like the day I got punched on the nose for getting between my mum and an abusive yob! Or the time when the kids were caught burning hedgehogs alive and leaving them in the gutter for fun. We were burgled three times in as many years and often felt acutely the spiritual battle in which we were engaged. I had many opportunities to sing and talk about my faith even though things did not really crystalize for me until I was sixteen and felt a call to full-time ministry. Preaching engagements came thick and fast along with more interesting experiences. I'll never forget the deaf organist who would always play one extra verse to each hymn! And the time I dropped the offering plates, sending them spinning across the floor. Or the time I tripped up the steps to the pulpit and the first the congregation saw of me was my two hands appearing through the front of the pulpit as I desperately tried to save myself from falling! Those were the days.

I applied to Spurgeon's College to train for the Baptist ministry and was told I should get work experience for three years first. I left school and got a job as a junior reporter on a local newspaper. I was in charge of the obituaries and tea making! The best thing I ever covered was a beauty contest! My wage was around £5.50 a week and I was to get two other jobs before finally starting my college course.

After a four-year course at Spurgeon's I gained a Diploma in Theology through the London University and started at my first church—South Ashford Baptist Church in Kent. My wife, Sue, whom I had married during my college course, and I settled down in our new manse and were there in ministry for five years. By this time we had two daughters: Rebecca and Sarah Jane. In 1978 I felt a call to specialize as a youth communicator/musician. With no 'package deal' in terms of a home and income, we were determined to prove God's power in a front-line situation. Six years, four house moves and endless miles later, we became linked to the Millmead Centre Baptist Church in Guildford where I have been one of the full-time staff pastors responsible for youth. After three years of ministry at Millmead, I am now in a more specialized communications ministry. There has also been a new addition to the family—a son called Thomas.

Briefly, that is my story, and I'll be using some of these experiences to punctuate truths for today's young person and anyone working in the youth sub-culture.

# I

# *Beating the Hell out of Sheerness*

'You've got a lot of bottle to play that thing in here, sir!' The time: 1979. I had just started out on the road to discovering the amazing potential of a schools ministry. The place: an unsuspecting sixth-form common room somewhere in the South of England. The 'thing': my new ovation six-string guitar, which I managed to drop on its first performance. It has never been the same since.

I rewound my memory banks to the day when I had my first brush with the owner of the ears on the receiving end of my twanging guitar. It was 1966 (ouch!), and with a low-slung Broadway solid electric guitar, which cost around £7.14s.6d. (secondhand), and my supercool sixties image, complete with adequate haircut and sideburns, I hit the headlines in the *Sheerness Times Guardian*!

It took me completely by surprise! I never thought I'd be shot at verbally by someone I was supposedly representing! Here was a clergyman going public on the evils of 'beat music' and the audacity of young whippersnappers claiming to be communicators of spiritual truth. There's nothing new under the sun! We are nineteen years on and the guns can still be heard in the distance from time to time, drawing attention to the so-called 'evils' of contemporary Christian music. More of that later!

11

The plain fact is that this minor incident had a major effect on me personally and indeed sparked off a controversy which was to rage for weeks on the letters page of the local rag! It started like this:

### 'Beat Group Bid to Save Church'

'The Victory Side'—the Island's own gospel beat group—has been called in to save Queenborough's ancient Congregational church. Dwindling congregations in the past years have necessitated this move by organist Mr Harry Poppleton and lay preacher Mr Colin Steele....

It came to a conclusion like this:

### 'Victory for Beat Group'

News of the services conducted by the Island's gospel beat group, 'The Victory Side' at Queenborough Congregational Church on Sunday, was flashed across Britain over the BBC Home Service on Monday....

The controversy in the middle went like this:

Sir, it is possible that your news item, 'Beat Group Bid to Save Church' could be misconstrued by a casual reader...I would like to point out that a policy of directing one's efforts to one small section of the community to whom too much attention is already paid—the teenage community—could well drive away members of long standing who have supported the church loyally. *(Rev P. E. Gee)*

I cannot understand why a minister, who obviously had found the answer and has a good congregation, first-class choir, etc., should bother himself about a group of young men who are trying to follow Christ's teaching. *(A 'Fuddy Duddy')*

### 'Beating the Hell out of Sheerness'

Sir, my efforts to set the record right as far as my own church is concerned, regarding the place of 'beat' services in our area, and the denial of the fact that we are dull and lengthy in worship, seems in danger of becoming a first-class argument. I believe the church is basically a family...so the teenage element must be prepared to forget the dominance which it has in the world outside by virtue of its high purchasing power, bizarre costume and uncouth appearance *(Rev P. E. Gee)*

Letters like these appeared in the paper for several weeks, some supporting the way we were trying to reach the kids on the street with the good news about Jesus, and others supporting the more traditional view of the clergyman.

### Feeling got at!

Things happen when you feel 'got at'. You can feel threatened and either retreat and run, or fight back, overstating the case to make your point. It could make you feel a failure and think that this situation now proves that what you thought about yourself all along is in fact true—you are a fat slob! You can spiritualize it and see it as an attack from the enemy who wants to hamper your plans to change the world for God. You may look objectively at the situation and use this negative to produce a positive—to become a learning exercise.

My own response to this reaction against what we were attempting was to take it personally. This resulted in a mixture of defensiveness: 'But we did it because...' coupled with unpredictable bouts of aggressiveness: 'Who cares anyway!'

The whole incident convinced me of certain basic truths which at the time I could not have defined clearly, but in later years have been able to identify.

1. I realized that there was a desperate need to break through the religious jargon which had so successfully camouflaged the Christian message and relegated it to church buildings only.

2. We must never write off so-called 'fuddy duddies' in the church who cannot identify with certain musical styles, but rather must learn to communicate with each other and find mutual strength and encouragement even inside the differences.

3. We must not be afraid to explore new forms of communication if they accurately and genuinely express something of the character and purposes of the God for whom we live.

I resolved that if ever I were to become part of the 'church system' that I would seek to reverse many of the unhelpful and indeed 'worldly' mechanisms which have clogged the works and paralysed our witness to the world. That attitude seems presumptuous when I examine it now, but nevertheless it became one of the driving forces of my life. For I could see evidence of a dying world and a church impotent and inadequate—a contradiction in terms. For if the church is truly the church, it will demonstrate the life force of God himself. It will speak with the authority of a shout, not the shallowness of a whisper.

### The deadly trap

'Tron Deadly Discs' is an addictive television game. Your man stands in the middle of the screen on a grid and suddenly the bad guys come in from the sides with their deadly discs. You are in mortal danger. You can steer your man out of the way of these flying missiles and, with your finger on the button, wait for your opportunity to 'get' them. The more of the bad guys you get with your deadly discs fired in retaliation, the more points you can score. The tension mounts and the game gets more and more involved until you end up in a frantic struggle for survival. Your ultimate aim is to get as many points as you can before they finally do you in. And get you they will! It's a 'no win' situation. That's the name of the game.

Does that sound familiar? We all play the game within

the brackets of our birth and death, and spend our lives working out how to win, knowing all along that in this game, there are no winners. The good news is that God has broken into the 'grid' of our existence in the person of Jesus Christ. He came to release us from the deadly trap of playing the game that nobody wins.

Beating the hell out of contemporary society is where we are at. Setting up the kingdom of light where once there was darkness. Showing young people the freedom that can be found in following a Jesus who broke into the 'system' and came out a winner!

## Exposing the persuaders

The influences that lure young people into 'the game' are numerous. Formative thinkers over the years have affected the drift of attitudes, lifestyles, life goals and ambitions. People like Herbert Marcuse, whose emphasis became known as 'The Great Refusal' influenced thousands as the 'hippy movement' was born in the States. Young people were taught to say 'No!' No to law and order. No to the establishment. No to religion. No to their parents. They would drop out of society and form 'communes'. Herbert Marcuse lecturing in Europe said years after these events: 'I taught this generation how to say 'No!' The biggest regret of my life is that I gave them nothing to which they could say 'Yes!'

The French philosopher Jean-Paul Sartre said that we have to make some judgements in order to live, but at the same time we find it impossible to make them: 'Any morals are both impossible and necessary.' He taught that the most important thing for life was to make your mark on the world. You could do that in any way you want, but life has no ultimate meaning beyond this.

Albert Camus, another influential philosopher, wrote a book called *The Myth of Sisyphus* in which he retells the classical story of a man rolling a stone up a hill. When he gets to the top of the hill, the stone will have grown bigger because it would have collected other bits of material on the way up. But having reached the top the man must watch as his stone comes crashing down the hill, smashing in pieces before him. He starts the process over again—and again, and again....

Modern philosophy, which has had such an influence on the way we think, is empty. It preaches that life is a circle. There is no meaning. We are all losers in the end.

Other world views have also influenced modern society, none more than humanism in its various forms. Man is god. We can survive. We control our own destiny. We have walked willingly into the deadly trap from which there is no escape.

Media bombardment has carried us along the deadly route, giving us a false sense of security but actually creating a world of illusion, where reality and fantasy merge in a confusing mismatch of fact and fiction. 'Compassion Fatigue' is the new disease as we watch endless scenes of violence and perversion, dulling our senses, hardening our hearts.

Stanley Kubrick's film, *Clockwork Orange*, a futuristic saga of murder, maiming and rape, triggered a spate of court cases where those accused of various atrocities claimed they had been influenced by the action on the film. This was in the early seventies. In the last fifteen years, the evidence that media communication in its various forms actually affects the way people act, has been mounting. The *Daily Mail*, involved in a campaign against video nasties, stated: 'Children swap horror stories from video nasties in the playground jungle.' The *Daily Express* in a similar voice said: 'Children who once marvelled at Mickey Mouse are now hooked on horror, while their parents are often unaware of what is going on—or couldn't care less.'

Dr Clifford Hill, Christian sociologist says: 'We may be priming a time bomb which will explode in the midst of our society.' A report commissioned by the Department of

Education and Science called 'Popular TV and School Children' expressed genuine fears that our children are being exploited and damaged by the things they watch. Here are some of the quotes from young people interviewed: 'I like JR because he acts so cool when things go wrong. And I would like to have his money as well as his power' (girl of thirteen). 'Violence is now another word for entertainment' (girl fourteen). 'My favourite programme is *Minder*. Each programme is packed with fighting, swearing and women' (boy fourteen). 'One of the major forms of corrupting a child is letting him see physical and verbal violence as an acceptable and everyday occurrence' (girl seventeen).

By the age of seventeen, the average American teenager has logged 15,000 hours of watching TV—the equivalent of almost two years day and night. The average figure for Britain is four-and-a-half hours of TV viewing per day. On the 2nd April 1981, Peter Greig wrote a feature article for the *Daily Mail* which was headed: 'Is it any wonder John Hinckley tried to kill the President?' He says:

> How ironic it is that the first US President to be made in Hollywood, narrowly escaped dying through a spin-off from that same dream factory. I should say nightmare factory.... Can anyone really be surprised? Surely when you think about it, the whole pointless assassination attempt on President Ronald Reagan by 25-year-old John Hinckley suddenly seemed sickeningly logical—even inevitable. Simple common sense— no psychological training is needed—indicates that such a film must prey on disturbed minds and produce and inflame an uncontrollable reaction. 'Taxi Driver' was an incitement to violence....
>
> Allowing Hollywood and its imitators to capitalise on brutality, is as perilous as handing open razors to potential suicides, pressing loaded guns into the hands of people swaying on the margin of murder, or giving disturbed directionless unfortunates a long glossy seminar on rape and violence....

More recently the *Daily Express* reported in its October 17th, 1985 issue, the findings of a fifteen strong team of experts commissioned by an all party group of MPs and Peers. They were asked to investigate the link between screen violence and behaviour. Made up of doctors and educationalists, they went on record as saying, 'The evil new menace is bigger than the drugs problem.' The newspaper article starts off, 'Sickening video nasties are turning out a new and horrifying generation of children who are hooked on violence.' From surveys done, it seems that neary half the children in the country over the age of six have seen horror films like, *Savage Terror* and *Zombie Flesh Eater*. Actual cases are cited in the 181-page report like: gang rape of a school girl based on a scene from the banned film of a rape victim's revenge, *I Spit on Your Grave*. A five-year-old who sadistically attacked his pet after seeing a violent video. There are quotes from children such as this one from a four-year-old girl: 'Mummy let me watch a nasty film last night and now I know all about sex. It's when a big man knocks you onto the floor and gets on top of you and you scream because it hurts.'

In the report *Children and Television* published by the National Viewers' and Listeners' Association, it says:

> Millions of children between the ages of 11 and 15 are watching programmes described by the Broadcasting authorities as 'adult'; that they have therefore seen many 'X' films, many 'Plays for Today', much of the adult violence which is now causing so much concern; have heard in their homes via television, obscene language, coarse blasphemy and watched explicit sex. The effect of this upon the minds and emotions of the children is incalculable.

The Tory Party chairman in November 1985, Norman Tebbit, said that the permissive society was to blame for the current outburst of violence and crime in our nation. He said that TV producers would have to pay more attention to the effects of their programmes on impressionable people.

It wasn't until Autumn 1987 that the public became aware of any real attempt on the part of producers to at least look at the problem more seriously. At the time of writing we wait to see what, if anything, will come of this new review.

## The backlash

There have been several significant 'revolutions' triggered by the kind of atmosphere generated by the 'hidden persuaders'.

### 1. The music revolution

Back in the fifties rock 'n' roll hit the big time with artists like Bill Haley and the Comets, Gene Vincent, Jerry Lee Lewis and, of course, Elvis Presley. In the mid fifties, 3,000 'teddy boys' went on the rampage through the streets of South London. Young people were being 'liberated' from the bondage of parents.

The 'Swinging Sixties' introduced 'Beatlemania', and youth culture began to have a real impact on the adult world. Over the years styles have come and gone, but perhaps the most significant in recent years is the punk movement. Dick Hebdige in *Subculture—The Meaning of Style* says:

> No subculture has sought with more grim determination than the punks, to detach itself from the taken-for-granted landscape of normalised forms, nor to bring down upon itself such vehement disapproval.

Peter York in *Harpers and Queen* said:

> There's a struggle going on! Little girls shoving safety pins through their ears and the posturings of nasty pop stars swearing on television are the outward and visible signs of an inward and spiritual crisis.

## 2. The fashion revolution

In the mid-sixties Mary Quant was asked where she thought fashion was going. 'Sex,' she replied. The young people were the people who counted and looking good was the thing to do. Rudi Gernreich designed the body stocking and topless swimsuit. The mini skirt became a must. The hippy movement brought with it beads, bangles and bells and the trend was, 'Let it all hang out!'

In 1967 the Beatles opened a boutique in London's Baker Street and sold Indian dresses. In 1969 the mini went out and the midi came in, boosted by the film, *Bonnie and Clyde*.

From that time on in the fashion world, anything was acceptable—unisex clothes, 'hot pants', transparent shirts, space age metal gear. The arrival of 'anti' fashion with the popularity of denim jeans has stayed with us till today, making this a sign of the biggest economic and social change in a long time. Fashion formed the 'exterior' look of the new liberated young people.

## 3. Sexual revolution

With the advent of the pill, the sexual revolution got under way and the permissive society took hold on the nation's youth. 'If it feels good, do it!' became the slogan for the 'hip' generation. Many have found this course of action heartbreaking, with broken relationships littering family life and causing so many personal problems. Dr Joyce Brothers in *Time* magazine wrote: 'We're not as swinging a people as we think we are. People found that instant sex is about as satisfying as a sneeze.'

Love with strings attached has ruined the lives of thousands. The tide is now changing and we are seeing a new evaluation of what love really is all about. In the United States, in the last five years, the number of women having pre-marital sex has fallen from 80 to 50%. The number of students living together has halved. (Source: Dr Nancy Clatworthy, an Associate Professor of Sociology at

Ohio State University.) The God who invented sex also gave us guidelines in order that we would enjoy to the full this beautiful gift.

It is not within the scope of this book to deal in depth with these responses but simply to draw attention to the responses that there have been in the battle to get people hooked for life.

In the *Daily Mail* on January 8th 1985, Elvis Presley's 50th birthday had he been alive, one man was quoted as saying: 'Elvis lives in my heart.' Another said: 'My wife and I have our bedroom dedicated to him, with lots of pictures on the mantlepiece, a five foot framed picture on the wall and two statues of him by our bed.'

There is a gaping wound in society personalized by all the lonely, hurting people, too afraid to let on. When I stood in that classroom mentioned at the beginning of this chapter, with my guitar slung round my neck, and looked beyond the facade, the sniggers and the 'cool' comments of the pupils, I saw a generation of young people bombarded from all sides by pressures threatening to destroy them.

Having travelled extensively for six years and worked in all kinds of situations from the streets of London to the Royal Albert Hall; from pubs and clubs to a regular slot on television; from prisons and institutions to schools and colleges... I know we have the answer.

Beating the hell out of a sick society is our business, as the kingdom of light smashes the flimsy, superficial structures of a dying world, driving the darkness away.

# 2

# *Can God Make the Silicon Chip?*

I began the first chapter in 1979, my first encounter in a schools ministry. After six years in this kind of work you learn things! This chapter is all about communicating the good news to a lost generation.

## The big question

There have been several major changes in the human story in terms of man's environmental development. Changes which have vastly altered our relationships with each other, with our world, and have threatened to invade our relationships with God. The Old Testament, the first half of the Bible, is centred around one of these major changes. In Genesis 15 we read about the covenant agreement that God made with Abraham who was to become the father of a nation through whom all the nations of the world would be blessed. Genesis 12 records the devastating moment when God laid it on the line for Abraham, then called Abram: 'Leave your native land, your relatives and your father's home, and go to a country that I am going to show you' (verse 1). Abraham was on the move, and he and his family and generations after him lived a nomadic existence—in other words, they lived in tents and worshipped God in a portable structure called a 'tabernacle'.

We jump ahead through history a few hundred years and we find the people of God moving into the 'promised land', Canaan, a land flowing with milk and honey, or so they thought. The Israelite life was crude compared to the sophisticated culture of the Canaanites. This was when the first big change took place. The Israelites moved from being a nomadic people to a different lifestyle, that of being a settled community living in permanent houses inside city walls. It was a massive environmental change that altered their view of God. Previously, he had been the God of the wanderers who protected them from their enemies and supplied their needs. Now they lived in walled cities and relied on the land to produce crops for food. Before their wealth was judged by the number of sheep they owned, now it was by the amount of land they owned. Now they had houses to live in not the insecurity of a tent. The Canaanites who lived in the land worshipped the Baal gods. Baal means 'lord' or 'owner' and Ashtarte was the female equivalent. They were the fertility gods that made the corn grow and the seasons operate in the right order.

The Israelites had to adjust to a brand new way of life and began to ask questions about whether their God could cope with this new situation. The big quesion they began to ask was: 'Can God make the corn grow?' Their answer, influenced by their new lifestyle and environment, was 'No!'

They did not deny the existence of God, but they began to deny his relevance to their lives. He no longer fulfilled a functional role in their lives but became a religious obscurity. 'As long as Joshua lived, the people of Israel served the Lord... then the people of Israel sinned against the Lord and began to serve the Baals' (Judges 2:7–13). 'Where are the gods that you made for yourselves? When you are in trouble let them save you—if they can!' (Jeremiah 2:28).

The pressure of the culture into which they moved was

too much for them and they began the downward drift of compromise and false religion. The Canaanites believed that the male and female Baal gods came together in sexual union and that it was this that caused the right conditions for the earth to produce a harvest. Sacred prostitution was thought to be a way of helping this process on. The Israelites would turn to their God in times of military crisis, but for their new agricultural existence with reliance on the earth to produce the harvest then the Baal gods of the Canaanites worked very well.

Parents began naming their children after the Baal gods. Gideon, for instance, was also named Jerub-baal which means 'may Baal multiply', and two of Saul's children were called Mephibaal and Ishbaal. Later the names were changed to Mephibosheth and Ishbosheth—'Bosheth' meaning 'shame' (1 Chronicles 8:34; cf 2 Samuel 4:4).

'Can God make the corn grow?' God spoke through Hosea the following words: 'She [Israel] would never acknowledge that I am the one who gave her the corn, the wine, the olive-oil, and all the silver and gold that she used in the worship of Baal' (Hosea 2:8).

The words of the prophets in the Old Testament are geared to reversing this attitude and bringing back into the life of the people of God reality in their relationship to him and a purity in their approach to worshipping him.

### The silicon idol

Since the Industrial Revolution, we have been undergoing another massive change which is producing the same kind of effect. The question was, 'Can God make the corn grow?' The big question today is, 'Can God make the silicon chip?' Like those before us we are coming up with the answer 'No'.

There are many people within and outside the church who are believers, but who have no earthly relationship with the living God. We have made him one of the great throng of the unemployed. He is redundant in his world. We have usurped his authority and believe that man has come of age and can handle the world and all that is in it on his own. We are moving into a world where the silicon chip is the new focus of attention.

Michael Shallis, Staff Tutor in Physical Sciences at the Department for External Studies, University of Oxford, writes in his book *The Silicon Idol*:

> Putting faith in false idols has always dehumanised people, led people into blind alleys... in the last few years we have built idols of silicon and our increasing belief in them makes us all more inhuman.

He says we have been 'intoxicated by technological narcotics'.

An amazing story reported by Jane McLoughlin in the *Guardian* (November 1st 1983) tells of a mini-cab driver who had an affair with a computer. He is reported to have said:

> I used to stay on in the office to use it.... I'd ask it things like, 'Do you love me?', and knew because I'd programmed it, it always gave me the right answer. Although I knew what it would say, the fact that it printed it out by itself made me think there was really a relationship between us.

Geoff Simons in his book *Silicon Shock* (Basil Blackwell) says:

> Human relationships face many threats—unemployment, poverty, physical or mental illness, adulterous affairs etc., and we now see how computers can be added to the list. At the simplest level, computers represent a seductive focus of interest, an alternative commitment that can pull devotees away from friends, lovers, spouses....

The titles of the chapters in his book reveal much: 'The

machine threat'; 'The dehumaniser'; 'The alternative love object'; 'The War maker'; 'The omnipotent machine'.

*Sounds* magazine, the popular music paper, reported on February 18th 1984, 'Like sharks ten years ago, computers have taken over the world. Also like sharks most people are terrified of them.'

Technology and its advancement is not in itself wrong. It is when we fail to acknowledge the God who has given us the capability of incredible achievements, that we begin to live the humanist's dream that never comes true. And like the prophets of old who could see the collision course that is inevitable when men try to make God redundant, we need to recover a strong prophetic voice to our nation. Not only speaking out against the injustice and immorality that will tear the nation apart, but also demonstrating the life of God in every situation. Just like the story of 'fantasy land' where the robots, programmed to serve all the desires of their human masters, gradually rebelled and turned the tables on them, so in our day we are witnessing a reversal of roles. The 'things' which we have made to serve us, have become our gods. We are being conditioned and programmed by them in a kind of vicious circle. The highly-mechanized lifestyles we now live, cut through much of the personal human touch that characterized life before the Industrial Revolution.

To understand this is to understand a vital truth which is a prerequisite to effective communication. For too long we have tried to communicate our message about God with language that has presupposed a 'God framework'. We have retreated back into a 'belief system' that works well in theory, but has not convinced the world that we serve a living God and have a relevant message in the age of the silicon chip. The God who was necessary in the days before penicillin is now redundant. The God who supplied the needs of people before the days of social security and unemployment benefit, is no longer required.

## The picture emerges

To help underline the trends that are appearing in contemporary society, it is helpful to reveal at this point statistics compiled by the Central Statistics Office, and published in *Social Trends* (1985 edition).

Fifty-six million people lived in the UK in 1983. Almost 90% in England and Wales lived in urban areas in 1981. The number of people aged sixty-five or over has increased by over two million since 1961. The number of people living in one-parent families with dependent children has doubled since 1961 from 2.5 to 5%. In the UK 162,000 divorces took place in 1983; 20% of those involved one partner who had been divorced before, compared to 9% in 1971. Of all live births in 1983 in England and Wales 16% were illegitimate compared with 6% in 1961, while numbers of illegitimate births rose from 48,000 to 99,000. Employment prospects for graduates in the UK have improved slightly recently. Of all first degree graduates of known destination 49% entered permanent home employment in 1982/83 compared with 45% in 1980/81. Nearly 10% of those twenty-three year olds who were intereviewed in Great Britain in 1981/82 for the National Child Development Study, reported literacy problems. Employees in employment in the UK increased by just over one million between 1971 and 1979, but fell by nearly two million up to 1983. In 1983, 95% of manual employees were entitled to at least four weeks holiday whereas in 1961, 97% were entitled to only two weeks. In 1981, 690,000 in Great Britain lived in families with incomes below the supplementary benefit level. In 1983, 57% of adults held a building society account, compared with 15% in 1968. Nearly half of the 663,000 deaths in the UK in 1982, were caused by circulatory diseases. The number of licensed private cars in the UK increased from 6.3 million in 1961 to 15.9 million in 1983. In 1971 only 36% of adults in Britain had ever been abroad on holiday. By 1983 the number had risen to 62%. The Citizens' Advice Bureaux in the UK received almost six million enquiries in the year to March 1984, about four times as many as in 1971. The prison population is projected to increase by 12% between 1982 and 1992 compared with a projected increase of 2% in total population aged fifteen or over.

I know it is possible to come to a variety of conclusions using statistics, but it seems obvious to me from my own experience of travelling to many parts of the world, from the affluent West to the poverty-stricken Third World, that we in the West are in danger of missing a vital discovery. As the world becomes more dehumanized and impersonal, resulting in external affluence but internal poverty, we will bypass a personal God who made himself accessible, knowable and reachable in Jesus Christ.

e recently that if you were able to drive a car at a constant 50 mph in a straight line, you could drive round the world on the equator in twenty days—about 24,000 miles. Light takes one-eighth of a second to do the same distance. The distance to the moon is approximately 240,000 miles. It would take us 200 days to drive there in our car doing 50 mph. A rocket travelling at 25,000 mph would take four days, but light takes 1.3 seconds.

Our solar system consists of a sun and at least nine planets—the furthest known at present being Pluto. It would take our rocket seventeen years to get there, and light takes 13.7 days. The nearest star to planet earth, Alpha Centauri, is quite a long trip. It would take a rocket, travelling at 30,000 mph (which is faster than our present capability), 75,000 years to get there! There are thousands of solar systems in our galaxy. It takes light 100,000 years to get from one side of our galaxy to another. Yet our galaxy is only a pinhead compared to the rest of the universe!

We have a great God! He is far greater than the silicon chip! Far greater than the universe he has made. Yet he is concerned enough about individuals to come in the Person of Jesus Christ on an amazing rescue mission to save the earth. If we are going to effectively communicate and be true to the revelation of God in Jesus; if the word of God is going to become flesh in us and the lives of others; if we are going to demonstrate the power of God and show the relevance of the Bible to our world today, there are certain conditions that need to be met. We need to live transparent lives through which God can live his life. We need to promote healthy and loving relationships that demonstrate the power and character of God. We need to be open to what the Spirit is saying today in order to formulate definite strategies to bring down the fortresses of the enemy and set up the kingdom of God in dark places. We need to cultivate by the touch of the Spirit in every area of our lives, a genuine desire to give God the glory as we unpack the good things he wants us to share with the world. We also need an understanding of the culture into which we are communicating and an openness to examine methodology and to evaluate our effectiveness before God.

We will be looking at these things in more detail throughout the book. In the light of what has gone before in this chapter, we need to take a closer look now at how to communicate to the world of the silicon chip.

## Connecting with people

How do you connect with people where they are? The normal man on the street has no 'God framework' from which to draw a background understanding of what we are about. We assume too much in our communication, often beginning way ahead of where people are really at. Let's learn to rewind the tape to the point where a connection can be made.

I was once asked to speak to a group of lay preachers on the subject of 'Music in Worship'. As part of my preparation for this I went through a hymn book which is popular in many churches today, and then wrote down some of the phrases that are familiar to us and that we sing often in our church services. Here are some examples: *Heavenly lay* (try singing that in a school assembly and see what reaction you get!); *angel strains*; *train filled the temple*; *I tried the broken cisterns, Lord, but ah the waters failed*; *wormwood and gall*; *our mortal frame*; *thou didst note my working breast*; *and the cream of all my heart*; *though feeble their lays*; *with his seraph train before him*; *in blissful answering strains ye thus rejoice*; *ye who have gained at length your palms in bliss*; *his chosen band*; *for swift and gallant horses, for lambs in pastures springing, for dogs with friendly faces, for birds with music thronging, their chantries in the trees*; *for bread to stay our hunger*; *prophets enraptured*; *thine eye diffused a quickening ray*; *glorious throng*; *publish abroad* . . . and so it goes on.

Now I'm not advocating that we ban ancient hymns. What I am saying is that we need to examine carefully the language we are using and make sure that we are raising the Lord's name up and *not* bringing the house down by singing words that have humorous connotations to the uninitiated. If we are going to use old-fashioned language let us be aware of the subtle changes of meaning that many words have been through and let's explain the reasons why some of the great hymn writers wrote what they did in order to put the songs in their right setting, and the timeless truths in digestible format.

Let's also be open to new songs which speak of the depth of what God has done for us, not merely nice little ditties that have no real content. Let's pray for the Lord to raise up new hymn writers. If God can raise up men like Wesley and Newton, surely he can do the same today so that we can creatively express what he is doing in our time.

People ask, 'Can God make the silicon chip?' and often the church implies loud and clear, 'No, we serve the God of yesterday not the God of science and technology.' We confirm to many that our God is irrelevant by the irrelevancy of what we do and say. Sunday school lessons that provoke giggles because of style and content degrade the faith. Sermons, hymns and language that generates amusement disgrace the gospel.

Students have followed a custom on the old Hiram College Showboat, 'Majestic', of re-enacting old melodramatic plays while sailing down the Ohio river. Plays with titles like: *Ten Nights on the Bar Room Floor* and *Murder in the Red Barn*. The students faithfully present the plays as they would have been acted last century. They are full of tragedy with almost every conceivable misfortune taking place. They come across to the modern-day audience as hilarious comedy, but in the 1800s they received a very different response. Joyce Cary quotes Chester Nimmo who says:

> I was trembling all over. My face was wet with tears and sweat. I heard myself utter groans and smothered cries. It was all I could do not to shout out my sympathy and rage. In fact cries of anger and exclamations of horror did continually break out from the audience during the whole performance. The women especially gave vent to their feelings...one girl broke into loud hysterical sobs.

The same words produced opposite responses. Let's be careful we are not reinforcing the false view held by much of contemporary society; that we are irrelevant.

### Getting switched on

Communication is big business. Fred Silverman, President of NBC television in the US, helped the corporation overtake its rivals CBS and ABS in its viewer ratings with the following principles:
1. Make people laugh. There's enough tragedy in the world.
2. Start off with a star.
3. Stress the positive, not the negative.
4. Glorify the common man.
5. Familiarity breeds acceptability; forget originality.
6. Cartoons aren't only for kids. Don't be too clever.

7. If you're going to take chances take big ones.
8. Grab 'em when they're young.
9. Keep the plot moving—fast.
10. Hold 'em for the first ninety seconds and they're yours.

Without getting into the rights and wrongs of such principles from a spiritual and moral point of view, it is interesting how we in the church have generally taken an opposite approach:

1. Make people cry. There's enough frivolity in the world.
2. Start off with a failure.
3. Stress the negative, not the positive.
4. Expose the common man for what he is.
5. Familiarity breeds contempt; obscure is reverent.
6. Cartoons *are* for kids; be more clever.
7. Don't take chances—we can't afford it.
8. Grab 'em when they're young—they'll make good Sunday school teachers.
9. Avoid anything moving—fast.
10. Hold 'em for the first fifty minutes and they're yours.

We must learn the lessons of successful communication if we are going to show a young generation the God of the silicon chip.

'If you let a TV set through your door, life can never be the same.' So said the *Daily Mirror* in 1950. Arthur C. Clarke referred to the influence of television as 'more powerful than the bomb'.

The book from the major ITV series *Television* by Francis Wheen, quotes from some letters received by agony columnist Abbie van Buren:

Dear Abbie, what can be done about friends who drop in unexpectedly while we are watching our favourite TV programmes? We hate to be rude, but we would rather watch our programme than visit with them....

Dear Abbie, this may sound crazy but I need your advice. I am divorced and the mother of a sweet four year old boy named Ronnie. We were at home recently when an armed intruder confronted us. The man was gentle and he quickly put Ronnie at ease—he wanted only money and promised not to hurt us. We both explained to Ronnie that Mummie would have to be tied up for a while; he seemed to understand. After I was bound and gagged, Ronnie was told to turn on the TV and when the programme was over, about 20 minues, he could help me or call for help. I was taken to another room and the robber left. Abbie, my son spent the next three hours watching TV while I was bound and utterly helpless.

It is reported that a poor mother, when asked why she was replacing her black and white TV set with a colour one, replied, 'I don't want my children growing up not knowing what colour is.'

## Three principles

There are three general principles that we should allow to filter through into our whole approach to communication.

### 1. Incarnation

John wrote: 'The Word [Jesus] became flesh and dwelt among us full of grace and truth.' This is the first principle of communication. We must allow the Word to become flesh in us if we are going to be successful in our communicating this to others. God will not speak theories at us from a distance. He comes as an embodiment of his Word to show us the way. It's hard to explain to someone over the phone how to play chess. It would be much easier and effective to go round to their home and show them the game and how all the pieces move, etc. God comes to where we are and expresses his life. Now, he wants to express his life through his body, the church.

## 2. Involvement

We must, to use an old cliché, earn the right to speak. Unless we are really prepared to love the way Jesus loved, we have no right to preach at people. The gospel is made effective by Calvary love in action. Involvement may mean being open and vulnerable, listening and sharing lives together. It may mean, instead of being impatient for 'results', learning God's timing and approach. Involvement also means taking the initiative with people; it does not mean being pushy or invading someone's space. Things which have become stumbling blocks and developed into real hurts will surface naturally as we demonstrate the genuine love of God for people with no strings attached.

## 3. Infiltration

Simply being God's person where he has put us is a vital lesson we must learn. We all have a role to play, allowing the Spirit to flow naturally through us in daily situations through our attitude and approach to life's situations. We need to have a definite aim to 'influence' things for God. The deep sea diver needs a diving bell in the work that he does. The diving bell protects him from the pressure of the water which could easily crush him without this protection. But how come the fish are able to survive without this protection? The deep sea fish have a pressure pushing out from their body equal to the pressure pushing in from the outside. This enables them to stay in one piece! The Bible says, 'He that is within you is greater than he who is in the world.' We have the power of the Holy Spirit! Let's get out of the protection of our spiritual diving bells and swim in the deep waters.

Back in the sixth century there was a holy man who felt the only way to be 'in the world but not of it', was to build a tower with a platform on top of it and live there. For thirty-six years his essential supplies were passed up to him at regular intervals and he refused to come down!

Communicating to this world which is in such a desperate state, means firstly *incarnation*—doing it the way God did by coming in the Person of Jesus Christ; getting *involved* with the needs of the world in a personal way, and *infiltrating* right into enemy territory in order to win the greatest victory the world will ever see.

## Specific principles

There are specifics we need to deal with here to help us in practical terms with how to communicate.

### 1. Be visual not vague

What I have been trying to say throughout this chapter is that we live in a world which communicates most effectively through visual means. Most people cannot grasp abstract thoughts. We have made much of our faith abstract and out of reach, therefore, to normal people. We need to rethink our whole approach and learn to visualize what we say.

Overhead projectors have become widely used in a variety of situations to help communicate messages. Video techniques are being used to great effect in schools and colleges around the country. We have a video show format at my church called 'Soapbox Chat Show' in which we use a variety of ingredients including video clips, interviews, crazy stunts, music, drama and reviews—all designed to be more effective in putting across a vital truth.

### 2. Be daring not diluted.

Use shock tactics! We need to see much more straight talking when it comes to effective communication. I use a variety of approaches that blow away the 'myths' kids have of Christianity, and mostly I use the element of surprise. The 'Gun' story is probably the most famous. I tell a story about the day I found a gun in the grass at an undisclosed location in London. At first I didn't think it could be a real gun, but the more I looked at it, the more I realized it was authentic. So I got a friend of mine who knows all about guns to clean it up for me.

We got some ammunition and then on some private ground drew a target on a tree. Over the next four years, when I had any spare time, I'd be down there practising with my gun.

At first I could just about hit the tree from one metre! But the more I practised the better I became. Eventually I decided to test my skills as a marksman by asking my friend to stand with a stick between his teeth while I shot it out.

He agreed to do this and when the big day came quite a few friends turned up to watch. I raised the gun and fired. People could hardly believe it when the stick came flying out of his mouth.

When I have got to this point in my story I ask the audience whether or not they believe me. Usually about half the audience put their hands up. I then ask, 'Out of those who do believe me, could I have a volunteer?'

I then give the volunteer a matchstick and ask him to put it between his teeth and stand an appropriate distance away.

With great ceremony I then load and fire the gun (using blanks, of course!). The reaction to this story, if told with energy and conviction, is quite electric.

The application is obvious. Anyone can believe in something without getting involved in it. Anyone can believe the story about my great marksmanship, but to be the one who volunteers and comes to the front to prove his belief, that is totally different. Anyone can say they believe in God, but that is not enough. We have to trust God enough to get involved with him and prove our faith. That's what makes faith real, when it is put into action.

Be daring in communication. They will remember it.

### 3. Be relevant not redundant

Let's answer the questions people are really asking, not the questions we think they are asking. We need to scratch where they itch and grapple with the issues facing real people in the real world.

It is interesting how the popular daily papers report major incidents in a personal way. They always look at events from the perspective of ordinary people who are involved. Readers can identify more easily and quickly with a personal touch. Let's be relevant in terms of our personal application of events into the lives of our listeners.

### 4. Be creative not conservative

I don't mean be gimmicky or cheap. What I do mean is attempt to reflect the creativity of a great God. He wants us to use every means at our disposal to communicate his truth. We are made in his image and therefore have the potential to illustrate creatively the greatness of our God.

### 5. Be positive not pessimistic

It is obvious to others when we are unsure of our message and insecure in our faith. Let's move out confidently because of what God has done for us and because of what he has promised: 'I will be with you always.' I've seen folk involved with door-to-door evangelism with the disease known as 'the door-step droop'! They know for sure that when that door opens the person will not want to hear what they have come to say. Nine times out of ten, with that frame of mind and approach they are quite right! Think big. God is on our side!

### 6. Be selective not submerged

Say one main thing when you are trying to communicate to an audience. Don't try to cover too much ground. You could say that thing in a variety of ways, however, for example, through drama, dance, participation, simulation games, music, etc. Aim at the target and drive the point home.

## 7. Be directive not diffusive

You are going somewhere. You are hitting a target, moving towards a goal. You are painting a picture that will communicate a truth. There are different parts to the picture, but they are parts of one whole. Just as a building has a design and there is a definite end in view as it is built.

We will be touching on these things again with more practical illustrations as the book develops.

# 3

## *Shouting the War Cry!*

You can't pull the wool over their eyes! When you are standing in front of thirty-eight lively kids who, according to the harassed teacher, may break out into utter chaos at any given moment, it's no good giving them a Religious Studies lesson on 'Eschatology in the light of current world affairs'. It's the classic case of 'they know that you know that they know' there is no way they are going to listen. What now?

Then there is the common case of the inevitable 'God Slot' on youth club night in the church hall. It's the bit everybody dreads! They dread it because it seems totally unattached to where they really are. It doesn't fit into the flow of the evening and they feel the only reason you got them there was to preach at them. You dread it because you desperately want to reach these kids for Jesus but the hassle of trying to get them quiet every week is a struggle, and there doesn't seem to be any material around that will help you connect with *your* kids. You tried doing it at the beginning of the evening, but everyone started arriving late. So you shifted it to the end and everyone left before it. So you stuck it in the middle of the evening and everybody suddenly decided they needed the loo for five minutes while you were the one getting flushed! What now?

We've already dealt with some of the important principles of communication, such as: shock tactics, being visual not vague, being positive and creative, using thought forms and language that will connect with the kids, etc., but there is something deeper that we need to grapple with if we are going to be winners for God in these kinds of situations. There is an event recorded in the Old Testament which for me contains some of the elements that we need to apply and be aware of. The story of David and Goliath in 1 Samuel 17 is a blueprint for growth. Let's take a closer look at it.

## Act One

### 1. Scene One: Paralysis

Get the picture. Here are two opposing armies lined up ready for battle. There have been no fighting encounters yet because an ancient game is being played between these human competitors. It is called 'intimidation'! The idea of the game is to get your opponent to believe that he is a little squirt and hasn't got a leg to stand on. You do this by looking fierce, talking big, displaying an over-inflated self-confidence and looking as if you know what you are talking about. It's the kind of game you could watch in the Houses of Parliament, a school classroom, an average living room, the local youth club, a traffic jam, or even standing in a British Rail ticket queue.

So here is Goliath, nearly three metres tall, loaded with an impressive array of battle gear and obviously meaning business! He probably rehearsed his lines in front of the mirror earlier that day! The Philistines, whom Goliath represented, had been a continual stumbling block to the people of Israel, often creating havoc through their military exploits. When the Israelites first moved into Canaan under the command of Joshua, they did not encounter the Philistines. They gradually emerged as a national threat operating from their settlements along the coastal strip between Egypt and Gaza.

Goliath, playing the 'intimidation' game, quickly gathers an audience of spectators, each of whom thinks somebody else should get involved. It's strange that it is often the person who shouts the loudest and looks the most confident who wins the day! This is illustrated over and over again in political debates, TV chat shows, trade union meetings, family life and even church leaders' meetings! Those in the firing line will back down, sit down and shut down! All systems stop! Result: paralysis.

This is serious. The army of Israel, who have known and experienced the power of the living God in real life situations, are being paralysed by the threats of the enemy. Make no mistake about it, we are in a spiritual battle in the twentieth-century world, that is developing in influence and coming to the surface in a series of what John Wimber, the author of the book *Power Evangelism*, calls 'power encounters'. I don't want to fall into the trap of spiritualizing historical incidents in the Old Testament, but the parallels are obvious. Goliath is acting in the way our ultimate enemy acts: 'If you are supposed to be the people of God, prove it!' 'If you are who you say you are, why do you live in defeat?' 'If God is really alive, where is he in your life?' The threats go on. 'If' is the devil's favourite word. '*If* you are the Son of God, make these stones become loaves of bread'; '*If* you are the Son of God throw yourself down from the highest point of the Temple'; '*If* you are the Son of God, come down from the cross and prove it!' Jesus was never intimidated by the threats of the enemy, and by using spiritual judo tactics he left him floored every time!

The enemy wants to paralyse the people of God. Unfortunately he often succeeds. We have been made to believe that we have nothing to say to the world and even if we did have something to say 'they' would not listen. We have been made to believe that we are not fit to go into the world with the good news about Jesus because we are unworthy.

We have reversed the command of Jesus to 'go', and wait patiently for them to 'come' while the world drifts by lost and doomed. We have learned to live with our problems and have become paralysed through inactivity. Where there is spiritual life, the danger is that we become holy huddles of people eagerly passing the 'fruit' to one another, and forgetting the people outside who are suffering from spiritual starvation.

Wake up! We need not be intimidated and play the devil's game! We really do have the victory! We just need to claim it in every situation. Jesus died and rose again to break through the barriers of sin, death and hell so we can have confidence as his people to walk through the door he has opened.

There are different things you can do with a problem. You can ignore it and hope that it will go away. You can encounter it and be thrown off course by it, going in a direction you never intended to go. You can be frightened into retreat and back track down old territory which you have already negotiated in your life. You can be stopped by it and wander in no man's land for years of your life. Or you can claim the victory of Jesus in the situation and break through. We can win 'power encounters' simply by taking hold of the resources God has already given us and learning how to use them.

It works like this. When you come up against a barrier that is obviously from the enemy, go for a demolition job! We are not into taking soft options as Christians. We are into living dangerously and demonstrating God to the world! We need to learn the secret of launching out, breaking into unknown territory, becoming pioneers and expecting God to work.

Some books you read are full of success stories and you end up feeling you could never live like that. In reality, most of us have our struggles of faith, our times in the wilderness, our moments of defeat. But in all these genuine experiences of life there is the underlying truth that the living God wants to live in and through us making himself known to the world. In my work with young people I have discovered that having confidence in what God can do and an expectation of him actually doing something, really does work. In many situations I have had the privilege of watching God at work, restoring, healing, giving new life, empowering, challenging, and equipping. The Israelites were paralysed by threatening words. Don't you fall for it!

### Scene Two: Poverty

Here's David coming with provisions for his brothers who are professional soldiers in the Israelite army. His father Jesse sent him because he was worried about his sons on active service. I can imagine David on his journey approaching the camp, singing some of his favourite songs on the way like 'Come bless the Lord'. As he looks from a distance he sees a fascinating sight. The armies of Israel are running towards the battle line shouting the war cry, full of confidence in the victory of God.

I worked for three years before starting at Spurgeon's Theological College in London. Even though I wrote to them when I was sixteen feeling convinced that I was ready to hit the world and start the revolution for God, I needed to get experience in the real world! (I have never despised a theological education and I am grateful for the four years I spent at the college.)

I remember my first week at college vividly! Being first year students there were things we were expected to do by way of initiation! One of these exercises was to show how well we knew our college 'War Cry' in New Testament Greek. We had to stand on the table and shout! The English translation went something like this: 'Are you afraid? Never! Are you afraid? Never! We are going out to the battle front and will win the victory'!

Sounded great! Just like a lot of our war cries do. We sing words in church like, 'Onward Christian Soldiers'; 'Fight the good fight!'; 'Sound the battle cry!' and 'There's a sound on the wind'. We stand up at the right time, sit down at the right time, close our eyes, put our hands together or in the air and do all the right things, but often there is total unreality.

What travels at between 100 and 1,000 mph towards the earth and then up to 87,000 mph away from the earth? Answer: lightning. That's very interesting, but who cares in a storm! There is a technical, clinical, intellectual approach to things, and there is a personal approach. If our Christianity is all theology and no application into everyday life, we have nothing to give to the world. Young people are fed up with unreality. If this belief in God is real, let's see it work! There is an appalling poverty in our spiritual experience which shows up when our faith is put to the test.

So here are the Israelites shouting their war cry. But see what happens next. When they get too close to the real battle, they turn around and run back in the other direction. How do you think David might react to this? Perhaps he is thinking, 'Ah! A new battle tactic. Very good! They are pretending to retreat so that they can draw the enemy after them and suddenly they will turn and pounce!' David is expecting victory because he has a simple faith in God that expects that kind of thing to happen. After all, God is pretty good at winning, doing miracles and making the universe work. When he got the real picture, he must have felt utterly disillusioned. There is a lot of that kind of thing around these days. People get disillusioned with 'church' because what we say and what we do are two different things.

If we are going to connect with young people, we need to learn more than just the latest techniques in communication. We have to learn the art of demonstrating the power and love of God. When we can show that our words actually work and have an effect, we will be operating effectively.

## Scene Three: Presumption

David arrives at the camp and meets his elder brother

Eliab. Here now follows the 'ministry of the wet blanket'. Eliab wants to know what David thinks he is doing here with the 'professional' soldiers, when he should be back home looking after his father's sheep. How dare he presume to be there! Makes you wonder who really owned the presumption! Was it David, who thought he knew better than his brothers? I don't think so. He has come on his father's instructions to bring provisions for his brothers, not to take part in the battle. What about Eliab? Now there we could have a candidate! He presumed too much. He presumed he was quite capable of handling this situation compared to little brother David. After all, he was a professionally trained soldier with battle experience and knew how to handle weapons and obey orders.

It's surprising how we make up our minds about people and situations without knowing the full facts. How many people do you know who have been let down by others because of a misunderstanding or because they didn't fit. Let's watch out for the young person who doesn't mix very well and seems to be a loner. Effective youth work takes place as we learn how to handle people who are 'different'.

Then there are the battles between the older generation and the young people. They can have their youth weekend once a year, but they had better not introduce all those new-fangled 'gimmicks' into the services any other time! Then there are the young people saying things like, 'The older people don't understand us. They use a hymnbook that's totally out of date and wear gear that comes out of the ark!' When are we going to stop fighting each other and go fight the real enemy?

It was great to see the back two rows of pews filled with young people at a church I preached at. But it was even better to see them get up half way through the service and mingle with the older folk, making an effort to build bridges and make relationships. Our youth work will be more effective when we learn to build bridges and avoid 'the ministry of the wet blanket'.

## Scene Four: Powerlessness

We've all been in the situation where we feel totally dried up and empty. Youth club night comes round again, and we've already spent most of our waking hours dealing with the perennial problems kids get. There are times when we feel we want to run and hide!

Then there are the times when we face a situation that threatens to place us right out of our depth. We may have read all the right books, but the theories don't fit this crisis. There is absolutely no substitute for a daily walk with God to keep us updated on what he wants for our lives. When we live on past experiences of God we become 'yesterday people', unable to cope with the demands of today.

That's the picture we see with King Saul. He had been anointed King, had experienced the touch of the Spirit of God and had seen mighty victories in his life. However, in facing the present situation with Goliath, he is completely out of his depth, stranded in powerlessness, God's yesterday man. Powerlessness is the opposite to what God desires for us. He is not looking for spiritual supermen, flying around in an unreal world sorting out everything at the drop of a hat. He is looking for people who will risk stepping out into unknown territory to claim enemy-occupied ground for the kingdom of God. That's the kind of clout that young people want to be part of, not the wimpish image of powerless people dwelling on past glories.

We have all the resources of the kingdom of God at our disposal. So let's take the initiative. Let's see what is available to us in the word of God and act upon it with confidence.

## Act Two

There are certain things about David that stand out a mile and we need to take note of them in the way we operate.

## Scene One: Consistency

We get the picture of a man who is consistent and reliable.

In the turbulent world of young people, this is a quality which will win battles and produce fruit. In the fast-moving world of changing relationships and uncertain futures, when young people are finding their feet and often falling over in the process, it's a *big plus* to have someone you can trust alongside to help. It has been said that in the church there are two kinds of people: the pillars who hold up the church, and the caterpillars who crawl in and out! Well, I'm not suggesting we should all become immovable pillars or crawlers, but we do need a consistency which springs out of a genuine love for God and others.

This quality was demonstrated in David so that whether he was tending sheep in the field or fighting a giant, he knew God was on his side! This gave him a positive attitude in relationships and in his approach to seemingly impossible situations. Unlike Saul, he had a living, relevant faith in God that actually worked. This is what the world is waiting for.

## Scene Two: Courage

David did not beat around the bush. He saw the problem and the potential for a speedy answer to the crisis which was crippling the people of God. When he tried Saul's armour on, it did not fit him and he had no hesitation in discarding it and discerning God's method of dealing with the problem.

We are far too quick in assuming that God will use the same old methods and the same old approaches. We look at our contemporary situation through yesterday's solutions. Now there are some things that never change, like the truth of the gospel message, but as we've already explored, the way we say it must change with the circumstances. There is no other place recorded in the Bible that indicates God used the same method on another occasion to defeat an enemy. This was unique and David knew it.

We must identify our targets, choose our weapons, and hit the bullseye! We can only do that as we listen to what the Spirit is saying in each situation. No beating around the bush! That armour had been used by God on other occasions to win mighty victories, but this time it was relegated to yesterday. Is God saying something new to you about your operations? It will take a lot of courage to dispense with the security of familiar ways of doing things, and it may be of course that to stick with the old formula is right—if it is working, bringing glory to God and young people into the kingdom. If it doesn't work any more, break into new territory!

## Scene Three: Confidence

There is a brash kind of self-confidence which is common these days, but which is a camouflage erected as a cover-up to deep personal insecurity. It only goes skin deep. David displays a confidence based on past experience in the way God acts. We have every right and reason to have confidence as we step into demanding situations because of all that God has done, assuring us of his capability to work when our human resources run out. Indeed that's the time when we have the opportunity of witnessing a miracle! If we are going to build the right kind of confidence into our young people, they need to know how much God values them and how reliable he is. They will pick up these truths as we are consistent and confident in our walk with God.

It always fires me up when I encounter the misconception that you have to blow your brains out in order to be a Christian! There is so much evidence for Christianity that from a purely intellectual point of view the Bible is convincing (that is, if the subject is approached with an open mind). I'm often asked in schools to 'prove it', but even if you give a convincing list of proofs for believing in a personal God revealed in Jesus Christ and made known by the Holy Spirit, there is still a scepticism that smacks of humanistic brainwashing.

Imagine you have a bag with one piece of paper in it marked with the number one. What are the chances that you could take the piece of paper out of the bag first go?

Answer: a one in one chance! Brilliant! Supposing you have two pieces of paper in the bag marked 'one' and 'two' and you want to get them out of the bag in the right order first go? You would have a one in two chance. If you had three pieces, however, you would have a one in six chance of getting them out in the right order, because they could come out in one of six combinations: 123, 321, 213, 231, 312, 132. Using the mathematical law of random you can work out how many different combinations you could get from having ten pieces of paper in the bag. To get them out in the right order you would have a one in 3,628,800 chance.

Try reading Isaiah 53:4–9 to a group of people and then ask them who they think this is describing. Do not tell them you are reading from the Old Testament. If they are aware of the fact that Jesus was crucified they will immediately recognize what this is all about. However, this was written a long, long time before Jesus came! There are many pointers to the birth, life and death of Jesus in the Old Testament—well over 300 in fact! Are you good at maths? Supposing you had 300 pieces of paper in a bag marked one to 300. What are the chances you could get them out in the right order first time? In the light of the above figures, the number would be so big it would stretch for miles! Yet all of those things written about Jesus before he came were exactly right! No man could act out their birth and death with all the accompanying details. It takes more faith to believe that the men who wrote the Bible guessed these things than it does to believe that they were inspired by God. The odds are far too great for guesswork.

The same would be true of creation. It takes more faith to believe that it happened by chance than to believe in a personal creating God!

The Rubik cube was all the rage once. It has been worked out that if a blindfolded person was given the cube to solve, and was to make one random move every second, it would take him 1,350 billion years to complete. This is a considerably longer time than the age of the earth itself. The

chance against it all coming right is 50,000,000,000,000,
000,000 to 1. Professor Sir Fred Hoyle says, 'These odds
are roughly the same as you could give to the idea of just
one of our body's proteins having evolved randomly, by
chance.' By the way, there are 200,000 types of protein in
our cells!

And so the facts and figures could go on and on. The
evidence is overwhelming.

Josh McDowell has written an excellent book called,
*More Than a Carpenter* in which he deals with some of the
proofs for Christianity. In his larger book *Evidence that
Demands a Verdict* he deals with the subject in more depth.

We can be confident in our God and the truth of his
book.

However, David did not have merely an intellectual
understanding of God. His faith and confidence were based
on the fact that God had made personal contact with him
and was operating in his life and experience. That's the key
to confidence in God.

## Scene Four: Credibility

When these kinds of characteristics are seen in your life,
there is a credibility that takes shape in you which bridges
the gap between head and heart knowledge. We will win
the battles when we have this kind of credibility.

We ought not to be people shouting war cries if there is
no down-to-earth demonstration of the power of God in
what we do.

One day in a small community a minor tragedy occurred.
The local Town Hall caught fire and was burning down.
The local people were very concerned because this place
was the focal point of community life. So they all rushed
into their homes and emerged carrying one loaded water
pistol each. Then, standing in a great circle round the
burning building, they began to squirt. The firemen arrived
and asked the people what they were doing. They received
a variety of interesting replies. 'Some of us are getting on in

years and don't have much time to devote to the life of our town, and others are young and taking exams or involved with bringing up families. All in all people don't have much time these days. But when we saw the Town Hall burning down we wanted to help. We can't do much, but we feel we want to contribute something to help put out the fire.' The fire chief quickly dispersed the crowd with the words, 'Go home! You're getting in the way! This is no place for playing games with water pistols! This is the place for men and women who are trained for the job and ready to give their lives to put out that fire!'

Bridging the credibility gap takes consistency, courage and confidence in God. We are not playing a game. This is no part-time interest or hobby. We are dealing with the things of the kingdom, and only out-and-out dedication will do the job.

# 4

## *The Spotty, Swotty Years!*

'Don't let spots ruin your social life!' The warnings are
everywhere. One teeny bop magazine offers a free leaflet
called 'Teenage Acne Problems Answered', and a ques-
tionnaire asks, 'Which, if any, of the following have you
tried: Medicated soap? Antiseptic cream? Astringent
lotions? Are your spots worse in the summer, winter, spring
or autumn? Is there anyone you feel you can talk to about
your skin problem?' The danger is horrific. The consequences unheard of. The remedies fly around thick and
fast, but the problem remains the same. The dreaded spot
strikes again! One magazine suggests that 'a girl's best
friend is her spot concealer, because what gal can face the
world when she knows the world is looking at the Mount
Everest impersonation on her chin?' Of course, we all get
them at a certain stage in our lives, when our biological,
intellectual and emotional make-up is developing fast, but
that doesn't stop them being a problem—for many, *the*
problem.

These are the years when the 'communication gap' can
become a serious problem in family life as a new independence is now sought after by children. 'When I was
seventeen I thought what an idiot my father was. When I
was twenty-one, I was amazed at how much he had learned

in four years!' That seems to sum up the experience.

In this chapter we are going to look at the difficult period that occurs during the teenage years known as 'adolescence' and then see how we can learn to cope with this in our family life.

# UNDERSTANDING ADOLESCENT DEVELOPMENT

A lot of excellent material has already been written on this subject by people like James Dobson, so I don't propose to go into great detail in this section, but rather to draw out some personal observations that may add to the thinking in this area.

## Rapid changes

The big wide world suddenly becomes a viable option. The opposite sex begins to create vibes you never thought could possibly exist. Life seems to offer a new set of possibilities. That's not always the story, but when it isn't, it usually means something has gone wrong. Let's examine some of the rapid changes taking place in teenage years.

### Imbalance

There are regular patterns developing of what some have called 'cyclical emotions'. Recurring thoughts and emotional experiences that are forming a backdrop to real-life situations and can affect the way young people react and respond. They could be negative associations from the past—perhaps being abused or badly treated in family life, or the loss of a loved one, or the disappointment that comes when the person you have worshipped as a hero begins to be seen in their true light. These kinds of things can create the regular pattern of ups and downs often associated with adolescent behaviour.

## Illusion

With unstable emotions, young people are highly vulnerable to 'auto suggestion' and outside stimuli. Unreliable impressions given via negative encounters can create an unreal fantasy world of illusion that can lead to false assumptions, wrong decisions, misled conclusions and, therefore, wrong actions. It is not right to attempt to shield young people from every barrage and attack from 'the world'. Experience is the great teacher and there are some things better caught than taught. Sometimes the pain of self-discovery creates new possibility for growth, and realization of potential that could never come from all the good advice in the world. On the other hand, let's be firm in our stand against the manipulators, making money out of creating illusions that lead to guilt, despair and even desperation. We need to guide carefully without restricting growth—take time to listen without overcrowding the person—have a non-judgemental stance while at the same time being firm about the issues involved.

## Independence

In the advice columns of the teen magazines there are always letters illustrating the struggle for independence:

> I have always been made to go to church by my parents. Now I'm 14 and I want to stop going because I really hate it. I've tried talking to them but it always ends in a row. They make me feel terribly guilty. (*Just Seventeen*, July 15th 1987)

From the parents' point of view the struggle is to be able to let go of their children despite the dangers they can see around them. They must be able to do this, however, without giving their children the cold shoulder. This will give the children their best chance for survival as they begin to stretch their wings and test the air turbulence while at the same time feeling the love and security of parents who care. When parents let go, it is more likely that their children will listen. That is not to say that there should be no rules. Mutual respect is a vital part of learning true independence. A sense of responsibility must be a built-in standard fitting of any healthy outlook on life.

## Ideology

During these years of rapid change, it is natural that young people will be testing and trying ideas and thought forms they have acquired during childhood. They will be examining beliefs and deciding for themselves what is true and false. Again, any pressure applied at this crucial stage of questioning can only create resistance, hostility and rebellion. Young people need to make discoveries for themselves upon which to base their lives. It is true that their upbringing plays a vital role in shaping their lives, but if that is seen as having been restrictive, or the beliefs shared have later been found to be hypocritical, then crisis looms. We have all experienced these things in our own lives and we know of many who have wandered for years in the wilderness of 'self-discovery' only to find that their original basis for living was true all along.

## Identity

As the discovering process continues, so the adolescent teenager is measuring himself against certain criteria. This list will vary according to the perception of the young person involved, and will probably be influenced by the current trend of thinking about the value of people. It may look something like this: in order to be accepted you need...

　　(a) *Physical attractiveness*. As one magazine put it, 'You need friends to tell you what you should and shouldn't wear.' The adverts scream at us loud and clear: you must look good, have the right image, attract the opposite sex, keep fit, stay slim.... This of course is cashing in on the inferiority complex most teenagers seem to have about the way they look. In a recent survey, 80% of teenagers did not like the way they looked. This produces a continual striving after perfection; an unattainable goal.

*(b) Intellectual capability.* Parents who call their children 'stupid' all the time are building a framework for insecurity that will come out in later life. Many who cannot attain intellectual goals crash out in their own alternative world, inwardly believing themselves to be failures. They try to give the impression that everything is all right and they wanted it to be this way. There should not be that pressure on young people. Yes, they should be encouraged to work hard and do the best they can, but not to think that this attainment gives them worth in itself.

*(c) Material wealth.* More and more in our society the pressure is on to 'have, have, have'. Those who do not have, have not made it yet. So the person with the biggest stereo, the fastest bike, the largest collection of records, the latest fashionable clothes, is the person who has proved himself and is worth something. There's a difference between cash (or more likely HP!) value and personal value. One of the fastest growing problems among young people today is this 'desire to acquire' going out of control and then the backlash of repayments on HP or credit card having to be met.

*(d) Physical performance.* With the ever-growing popularity of gym clubs and body-building exercises, the race is on among the youth group to see who can turn out the best performance. Again, physical fitness and competition are not wrong, but when success and worth are measured in these terms we are sadly lost.

So the teenager is trying desperately to discover who he is. If the external rules are applied, he will continually be fighting to measure up. It's at this point where we need to encourage the acknowledgement of internal values springing out of our identity in God. That can often only come when young people see it in the lives of others rather than hear about it as some kind of nice idea.

## Illumination

These years are a time of growing self-awareness in every area of life. As the young person reacts, interacts, tests, explores and discovers, there will be this gradual understanding of certain things about them. The most important area of self-awareness is in their sexuality. As their bodies develop and grow, they will notice new emotions and sensitivities not known before. This can be a frightening experience if they are moving into unknown territory. We have always adopted the policy with our children, to answer their questions straight away, honestly and openly. We feel that if they ask the question, then they must be ready for the answer—and better to come from us than from behind the bike sheds at school!

The questions being asked by teenagers as they develop physically include things like: Are all these changes supposed to be happening? Is there something wrong with me? Do I have a disease? Am I different from other people? Why do I have pains in my breast? Why do I have to have periods and what should I expect to happen? Why do I feel guilty about the sexual feelings I have? Could I get pregnant without having sexual intercourse? Do some people fail to mature sexually.

Parents need to be supportive, honest, loving and caring during this time of illumination, when things are being put into the right perspective and new discoveries are being made. To interject with the wrong influence at this point can have tragic consequences. That is why it is criminal that the Gay Movement should get away with giving out literature to twelve- and thirteen-year-olds encouraging them to explore any feelings they have for the same sex. They need time and space to work through the natural feelings they will have for both sexes as things develop.

During this time of rapid change, young people need to have a self-worth, a sense of direction in life, a feeling of security that comes from knowing exactly where they stand. All this can come from understanding parents. But the state of our society today means that there are very few really stable marriages and a growing number of one-parent families. It's not surprising that the casualty rate of emotionally crippled children is on the increase. Ultimately it's our relationship with God that counts. He knows how we tick and he can supply all that we need to make us whole people.

## Powerful influences

I have written elsewhere about the 'hidden persuaders' and their effect upon the society in which we live, so I won't dwell on this heading. We do however need to make a reference to the fact that during adolescence there are powerful influences that can change the course of lives.

### Peer group pressure

The 'herd' instinct is a powerful one and it's very hard for anyone to stand out against the crowd and be different. There is so much talk about 'liberation' and 'do your own thing', but few people are really free. We are so affected by what others think and do. Scripture teaches in Isaiah: 'All of us were like sheep that were lost, each of us going his own way' (53:6). The peer group is an important part of the development of teenage life. It forms an identity unit and a bond linked to common interest which can be healthy. On the negative side, young people can be pressurized into being involved with all kinds of unreasonable behaviour patterns because that's what everyone says should happen.

### Media

As Cliff Richard released his 99th single, 'My Pretty One' in 1987, after twenty-nine years as a pop star, he was quoted in *Smash Hits* as saying: 'The songs I *don't* record are painfully obvious. They're either brutally cynical—which I don't want to be—or they're over-sexed.' When questioned why he had asked that his performance of 'Living

Doll' be taken off the 'Comic Relief' video, he replied:

> The 'f' word was flying about and I was thinking, 'They're videoing this!' Yes, the cause was good, but personally I don't believe that any means to an end is right. When we made the record it was straight down the line, fun and laughter and it sold a million. That proves you don't have to cause offence and embarrassment to be successful. I'm constantly proving it.

At the other extreme, Madonna, whose popularity and notoriety has grown rapidly in recent years, states quite blatantly in *Just Seventeen*: 'I knew that being a girl and being charming in a feminine sort of way could get me a lot of things, and I milked it for everything I could.'

The influence of the media during teenage years is blatantly obvious. It can be seen by the way young people imitate TV heroes, emulate pop stars, and model themselves on the latest dictated fashions. With the rapid advent of all night TV in Great Britain, those who have time on their hands will continually have their minds filled, dulled and exploited by the image makers.

When Leslie Halliwell, ITV's chief film buyer, resigned he said, 'I know people think I'm old fashioned. I only hope I'm wrong about the way in which television today is headed. The answer lies with the public.'

## Family

The greatest single influence on a life is, of course, the family. As has been stated, many of the responses, reactions and attitudes that come to the surface in later life have been formed during the early childhood years. At a time when family life as we know it is diminishing, those of us who claim to be part of God's family must stress and live out the importance of God's idea of the family. It is the strength of a nation and it forms the foundation of community and national life. However, children can be damaged for life by their home experiences.

David French, Director of the Marriage Guidance

Council which has had some controversial press over the last few years, has stated quite categorically, in the light of another 160,000 children with parents separating this year, 'Marriage is for life.'

The phenomenal response to Esther Rantzen's initiative in setting up 'Childline' has uncovered a problem that many suspected but none dared vocalize. The drift of moral standards in our nation has taken its toll and eaten away at the heart of family life. It's not too late to turn the tables. We must reverse the trend. It begins with your family and mine.

## Love and sex

'I'm sixteen and pregnant. I slept with a boy from school who is two years younger than me. We used a sheath, but it didn't work. Once he'd found out I was pregnant, he didn't want anything to do with me.' This is one of the tragically all-too-familiar kinds of letters you will find on the problem pages of any teen magazine. In the same magazine as this letter there was an article headed: 'Show Off. Some cotton undies are too good to keep under wraps. Be daring and wear your bra with jeans and a jacket. Go on, expose yourself!'

James Anderton, Chief Constable in the Greater Manchester area, hit the headlines in a big way in 1987 when he made comments about those most at risk of catching AIDS. He said that homosexuals, drug addicts and prostitutes were 'swirling around in a cesspit of their own making'. The day following the reporting of his comments the *Daily Mail* was swamped with letters of support. I suppose you would expect that of its readership, yet the response was staggering with people saying things like: 'At last a public figure finds the courage to articulate the views of millions'; 'Bravo, Mr Anderton, for saying loudly and clearly what most people are thinking'; 'People who criticise James Anderton and say we should not make moral judgements are only trying to treat the symptoms, without apparently even attempting to deal with the root causes'. Perhaps the most interesting of all the comments I read was: 'Now go one better and address an open letter to the Archbishop of Canterbury, the Archbishop of West-minster, the Moderator of the Free Churches and the Chief Rabbi, and ask them why they have not been thundering this message for months!'

The issue of love and sex has a high profile in all of our lives. I have already commented in an earlier chapter on the influence of the sexual revolution. Now with the threat of AIDS, which has received such vast publicity, we are being made to think about the consequences of casual sex as never before. 'We thought nothing of having casual sex and using recreation drugs,' said a young homosexual dying in a San Francisco hospital back in January 1987. Social Services Secretary, Norman Fowler, held his hand while the cameras clicked. In a year this man will be dead. Lynda Lee Potter, journalist, commented, 'He's one of thousands of AIDS victims who thought that sex without commitment meant liberation. Instead it turned out to be suicide.'

Dr James Dobson states the case clearly: 'An under-standing of real love explains the moral law, it does not abolish it.' And psychiatrist Dr John White says, 'Each time that sexual relations spring from casual encounters, something of their healing and life giving nature is destroyed.... Such relationships enslave and destroy.'

The vast pressures on teenagers during the adolescent years are frightening. With the word 'love' being made to be synonymous with 'sex', there has been created a totally distorted view of love. The gift from God designed to be a beautiful and fulfilling union between man and wife, has become a destructive force in the hands of man. When fourteen-year-olds are under pressure to sleep with their boyfriends to 'prove' their love for them, we are not only getting dangerously close to emotional blackmail, we are also witnessing the results of what the older generation has sown. May God forgive us.

There are different kinds of love exhibited in the world today:

*Conditional*. 'I'll love you if you do what I want you to do for me.' This is a common approach and although it rarely comes across like that, it seems this is the most familiar distortion of love we see. There are a lot of devastated people around us who have been hurt by others because they were used by them and treated like objects rather than as people.

*Contrived*. 'I'll love you because of your image/status/power/influence.' When I was seventeen I passed my driving test and bought my first car. Naturally I wanted to impress my girlfriend so I took her out for a spin down the motorway. The car was the classic Ford Zodiac and could quite easily do 100 mph. Another good thing about the car was that it had a column gear change and front bench seat. This meant that you could drive with one arm round the girl and look really cool! On this ocasion my friend came with his girlfriend and they followed us down the road in their car...a three wheeler! I felt really good! It would do my image a power of good on this day. You see, my car would easily do 110 mph down the motorway.

I drove at a fairly steady speed to begin with—not wanting to show up my friend and make him look silly. When you've got a car that will do 115 mph it does tend to make you rather confident! Suddenly it happened! I noticed this car overtaking me on the fast lane. It was my friend in his three wheeler, bouncing all over the road and having a great time. I never knew they could go so fast! It made me mad. How dare he overtake my car when I could easily do 120 mph and leave him standing! I put my foot right down on the accelerator and surprise, surprise, the cable broke! I drifted to a stop and I was shattered. My 130 mph car was out of action, and my image was in ruins.

When we rely on prestige, image, possessions or status to

make relationships for us, we end up with a contrived love
that is not real. A love that could change as soon as someone bigger and better comes along. But many people live
like that and relationships are made and broken with regu-
larity because of it.

*Consecrated*. There have been those who have died for
their nation, family and friends. There is only one person I
know who was prepared to die for his enemies! Jesus Christ.
'Father forgive them,' he said. 'They don't know what they
are doing!' As he hung from the cross where he paid the
awful price of sin and took the penalty on our behalf, Jesus
was displaying a unique kind of love that the early Christian
could not find a word for. So they found a new one: *agape*.
It means 'totally self-giving love'.

Jesus used the same word in John 13 when he said, 'Love
one another. As I have loved you, so you must love one
another. If you have love for one another, then everyone
will know that you are my disciples' (verses 34–35). This is
the kind of love that survives and is real. It has a wide
application. It can refer to the self-giving love we need to
generate in boy/girl relationships, husband/wife relationships, family life and relationships with neighbours and
friends. This is the love that will change the world.

Adolescence is a difficult, exciting, tumultuous, rewarding, adventurous, dangerous and stimulating time of life.
Love and sex are crucial issues to talk about with each
other. We must get it right. God gives rules not to limit and
restrict but rather to liberate and fulfil. Sex in the context of
the security of marriage is part of God's plan. He knows
how we tick. If you take the fire out of the confines of the
grate and put it in the middle of the living room floor, the
whole house burns down! Sex is God's gift, but only operates in the way God designed when we live by his guidelines.

The *Buzz* magazine survey conducted in 1987 revealed
an incredible number of Christian people with sexual problems. This surely brings to the surface a fundamental need
which is not being met. Leaders in the church need to put

on the agenda clear guidelines to help people in this area. We must not point fingers at people—that's like throwing the first stone. We need to tackle this problem with relevance and down-to-earth common sense.

## RELATING IN THE HOME

### Communication

We know the all-too-familiar morning scene in most homes around the country! Pandemonium! One of the children reckons he is glued to the mattress and can't get up for school today while the other has claimed the bathroom as her territorial right and refuses to come out until she is ready. Mum's rushing around the kitchen trying to get orders for the toast and bemoaning the fact that it must be someone else's turn today. Dad's got his face in the morning paper pretending to keep up with the news (while he is actually trying desperately to get his eyes open), issuing a grunt here and there in response to the conversation!

Because of the rapid pace of life these days, it is often true that the whole family rarely sits down to a meal together, apart from at weekends. This does not help the first rule of successful family life: communication.

I have often been involved with marriage guidance counselling and sometimes do the following. I will ask the couple concerned to come and see me together. I will then ask her to tell me all the things she feels are wrong with the marriage. When she has finished I will ask him to tell me what she has just said. Guess what? It turns out that he really didn't hear what she said at all. He interprets the conversation according to his view of things—and there is the communication gap. I then try the same procedure the other way round, and the same thing happens again.

Communication is the key principle in family life. We must encourage children to talk to their parents even when they don't feel they relate.

Young people, are you taking this in? You have to take the initiative! Don't be so high and mighty that you think you can stand alone. You have a responsibility to honour and obey your parents. You can't be expected to do that unless you have a close ongoing relationship with them. They may find it hard to relate to you. Why don't you make the effort?

Parents, it's your turn! Yes, I'm one too so I know the pressures! We have to make an effort to spend time with our children before we lose them. Showing an interest in them is vital. Attending school open days and encouraging our children when they are involved with activities outside of the home. Taking an interest in the work they bring home from school. Spending quality time with them to give them time to talk to us and for us to listen...all this is vital. Let's also make an effort to keep informed about what they are into so that we are not always trying to cross a mighty chasm when we talk to each other.

## Co-operation

We need to encourage our young people to get involved in their home life and not just use their homes as a boarding house! Get them to count up the number of times in the course of a year Mum does their washing, ironing and cooking. How many times have they shown their appreciation? A box of chocolates, a bunch of flowers or a simple thank-you card from time to time would go down well. As we learn to pick up on the little things, the bigger issues will begin to take care of themselves.

There is a lot of good material already written on family life [that I am recommending in the bibliography at the end of the book.] Do check it out and make further explorations into this vital area.

Ephesians 5 and 6 are all about relationship in the family and at work. The central core of the teaching by Paul here is in chapter 5: 'Do not get drunk with wine...intead, be filled with the Spirit' (verse 18). The rest of what is said hangs on that verse. If we really claim to be 'born again' and 'filled with the Spirit' then where is the evidence of that? Part of the outworking of this will be seen in our relationships as families.

# 5

## *Recycled Teenagers*

You've either got it or you haven't! If you haven't got it, all the trappings you can possibly think of won't give it to you. In my experience, you don't have to be young to work with young people—which is just as well for me! But you do have to be able to identify with them without trying to put on an act. There's nothing worse than older people trying desperately to look and act 'young' when it's blatantly obvious that they are past it. On the other hand I've seen older people relate to young people in a powerful and effective way.

In this chapter we are going to look at what it means to be a 'recycled teenager' (youth leader) and the basic principles of caring and counselling.

## HARNESSING THE POTENTIAL

### Leadership

#### (a) By definition

There are many different concepts of leadership depending on your school of thought, the circles that you are currently operating in, and your mood after another chaotic night at the youth club or deacons' meeting!

Leaders wear different disguises.

*The dictator* speaks and people crumble before the force of his authority (at least that's what is supposed to happen but rarely does). He claims to be able to get water out of any stone with his lead-filled truncheon and leaves boot-shaped indentations in every corridor he storms. With his cries of, 'Do this or else,' and, 'You *will* enjoy yourself!' his voice can be heard above the high decibel level of the youth club rock band. Normally the recipients of such an approach will discover all kinds of devious ways to avoid complying with instructions and even if they do jump to attention, the communication factor is a long way below zero. Sensing, rightly, that young people need boundaries, he tends to go to extremes, attempting to erect twelve-foot-high-barbed-wire fencing to help the kids feel secure. People often become dictators when all else fails. Normally, because of a genuine love for the young people, the dictator-style leader operates out of a frustration over his own inadequacy.

*The DIY leader* uses his position as a hobby. The young people are incidentals in the grand scheme of things. You can recognize this type by the bags under the eyes (or sometimes the eyes under the bags), the rocket boosters attached to the ankles, the 'Jim'll fix it' stick-on grin and the permanent worried look he wears. Never content to super-vise, he is always on top of everything and has often been seen clinging desperately to the 'big hand' on the local clocktower to try to retrieve the hours. The snag here is that everyone else uses the DIY leader as a hobby too! 'Jim, will you do this?'; 'I wonder if you would mind....'; 'There's nobody else who can do it like you'; 'Jim, you're the man who can save the world... and you've only got twenty-four hours to do it!'; 'We're all behind you Jim!'

Most dedicated, enthusiastic, energetic youth leaders have struggled with this problem, and it can be serious. If preventive action is not taken we have a 'burnt-out' situation rapidly approaching. Delegation is still the biggest lesson most leaders have to grapple with and it's not easy when you see your best laid plans being wrecked by the inconsistency of youth! There are ways and means, however, and this will be discussed later in the chapter.

The 'delayed echo unit' leader gets the news before everyone else, but is always one step behind. You can recognize him by the unusual way his head nods up and down as if attached to a spring. He is often seen walking behind his 'superiors'—and that includes most people—with a battery-operated cassette player in 'record' mode, catching every inspired utterance and command. The unique difficulty he faces can be observed at the Friday night youth club, for he will often be seen dangling by his strings from the rafters trying desperately to get his cassette machine into 'playback'. This kind of leader is useful to the 'boss', whoever that might be, because he can be sure that his ideas will always reach the 'shop floor' without he himself having to be tarnished by the 'riff raff'. The boss is usually a good chess player. The 'delayed echo unit' leader has a basic problem—he isn't a leader!

The 'Master of Ceremonies' leader keeps the action going! His catch phrase is, 'And now....' You can easily identify him because he is the one with the cotton wool stuck in his ears and the far away look in his eyes. This betrays the fact that he is probably somewhere else. This youth leader is usually very thin, because he is always jammed between one event and the next. He is also very lonely because most people are doing something else. The problem here is that, with all the good intentions in the world, simply laying on 'activities' does not ultimately fulfil the needs of the young people and they begin to drift.

The 'executive'-type youth leader has a Filofax, Samsonite briefcase and looks like Frank Sinatra. This is because he is always singing 'We'll do it my way!' to the tune of 'You'll always walk alone'. He is chairman of numerous committee meetings where 'any other business' is the main item on the agenda. This is so that controversial issues can be raised without members having had time to prepare a response, thus leaving the way clear for him to make a devastating and convincing speech that will normally win the day. If he talks long enough he gets the vote so that they can all do what they've been waiting for—have a cup of tea! The executive-type youth leader usually has such long legs that he just walks right over the young people without noticing them.

The list is endless. There is, of course, a little bit of good in most 'types'. Usually it got distorted and adapted when the 'wrong' lessons were gleaned from the grim battlefront of experience.

A youth leader is called upon to exercise a variety of abilities. Planning, organizing, co-ordinating, trouble-shooting, communicating and building. He must be alert to latent potential in people, ready to be firm on issues worth defending, able to listen and to hear accurately what others are saying, flexible enough to shift emphasis when plans are not working, amenable enough to be 'one of the boys' (or girls) while at the same time keeping a finger on the control button. Let's now look at some of these abilities.

## (b) By demonstration

Spiritual leadership stands or falls on this basic principle. Are we living out what we preach. You are in one of the most vunerable situations in the church because young people cannot be fooled. They will pick up quickly on hypocrisy, double thinking and unreality. They may be that way themselves, but they have high standards for their leaders! That's the name of the game. Spiritual leadership ought to be recognized by demonstration and not merely by appointment of those in authority who know nothing about the youth scene. Gifts will come to the surface as potential leaders are exposed to different situations. It needs a dis-cerning mind to see the possibilities and encourage the opportunity.

## (c) By direction

As leaders we must formulate goals and target areas. Do this with your young people. Do not be so immovable that you can't shift once strategy is laid, but at the same time, stick to a course of action if that's what you feel as a group is right. Young people can move up and down very quickly. It's part of their natural development as they go through adolescence. So at this stage, strong leadership by direction has a positive input into their lives.

## (d) By delegation

For the health of the youth leader and the group he leads, this is a vital aspect often overlooked or ignored. We need to encourage people to grow by experience, exploration and self-discovery. It might be quicker to do the job yourself, but in the long run you will achieve much more if others are involved. Here are a few suggestions of ways to get the best out of people.

*(i) Be a receiver as well as a transmitter.* Too many of us know how to give but not how to receive. A successful youth leader can do both. Some of the most precious moments I shared with my youth group were the times when they prayed publicly for me. We discovered a new depth of relationship because of this strange kind of vulnerability. You won't lose their respect, you will gain their friendship. Don't always be giving out your ideas to them. Get them to use their minds and creative ability to think things through for themselves. By all means give direction and share your own feelings about things, but steer and let others use the map.... with a watchful eye from yourself, of course!

*(ii) Allow for mistakes to be made.* Help people to learn through their mistakes and persevere with them when it seems difficult. Do not allow them to feel threatened, but encourage and give a gentle push now and then.

*(iii) Never criticize an individual to the point where he*

*will never do that job again.* That is a devastating experience for many young people who have been through times of being intimidated and patronized to the point where they simply switch off and close down.

*(iv) Do not force your methods of doing things onto them.* Make suggestions, don't issue commands. Perhaps they have a better way, but if not let them discover for themselves.

Here are some suggestions to help in the actual delegation process, bearing in mind the above criteria.

*(i) Contact.* Make a personal approach to the young person concerned. Try to remember names. Whenever you hear a name repeat it over a few times in the conversation and then at the end of the day, write down all the names of the new people you have met.

*(ii) Confidence.* You must gain the confidence of your helper. This will happen if as a leader you are always consistent and above board. Honesty and integrity are vital. Make sure you keep promises.

*(iii) Convince.* The young person must feel that this is a worth-while exercise and is part of something bigger. Take time to explain and encourage. Build self-worth and value into the job in hand.

*(iv) Contribute.* Encourage their development by making sure they have adequate knowledge of what they are doing. If training is needed, see that it is provided. Clearly define what has to be done and keep the responsibility ultimately on your own shoulders so that you are in touch with the developments moment by moment.

*(v) Channel abilities into areas of larger responsibility.* This is a faith-stretching exercise and will bring growth and fulfilment as we work alongside them in this exciting process of self-discovery.

*(vi) Commend and encourage them all along the line.* Never close a door without opening another.

## (e) By dedication

Jesus' view of leadership centred around the concept of servanthood. As Jesus bowed at the feet of his disciples and washed them, he was displaying the greatest form of leadership ever known. He who had the right to assert his rights, waived them. If we want to be leaders, we have to learn how to serve. We are not leading from a position of privilege, but with the backdrop of the grace of God. We are not in a competition to see if we can impress with our abilities and gifts, but rather we are seeking to explore with our young people the best way of discovering and using the gifts God has given.

# DELIVERING THE GOODS

Youth leadership involves working with people. In this section we are going to take a look at ways of helping young people and the reasons behind some of the problems.

A lot has been written about caring and counselling and there is no way, in the space of one section of a chapter, that we can hope to deal adequately with this vast subject. It is my intention to take an overview and home in on the key principles which I think will be a practical help.

Corrie Ten Boom tells of an amazing experience she had when encountering an ex-Gestapo officer. He had carried out atrocities in the concentration camp where she was sent in the second world war. She survived the horror, but the scars remained and she found it impossible to show love for this man. However, she goes on to tell how the Lord performed an incredible miracle of inner healing in her life as he gave her the ability to love him.

Very few of us are likely to have been through that kind of experience as a test of love, but we are all called to care for one another. Jesus said, 'By this will all men know that you are my disciples, if you have love for one another.' It is the supreme evidence of the presence of God in a person's life.

Here is an exercise that is good for every leader to do at regular intervals. Whether you are a pastor, youth leader or in some other responsible role dealing with people, check this out.

*How well do you know your people?* (Grade yourself between one and five according to how well you know them.)

A.    I know the names of all the young people.
B.    I know and use their nicknames.
C.    I know where they live.
D.    I have been to their homes.
E.    I have met their parents.
F.    I know their families.
G.    I know about their boyfriends/girlfriends.
H.    I know where they are studying.
I.    I know what their interests are.
J.    I know what exams they are taking.
K.    I have joined them in their spare time activities.
L.    They have been to my home.
M.    They feel they can talk to me about anything.
N.    I really love our young people.
O.    There is a sense of belonging in our group.

I picked up a book recently called *First Aid for Hypochondriacs*. It claims to deal with things like: 'The importance of panic in any crisis'; 'How to tell if your heart has stopped'; 'How to say, "I'm sick!" in 20 languages'; 'Tips for taking your pulse in public'; 'How to help yourself when everyone else is sick of you'; 'Easy-to-follow patterns for impressive bandages'; 'Emergency action for those eager to hear the worst and make the most of it!' This last one sums up this tongue-in-cheek book which could also be applied to the spiritual hypochondriacs.

As we look into the vital aspects of expressing our love

and care for one another, and techniques of uncovering problems and dealing with them, we are not talking about digging into people's lives for the sake of it. We are not talking about bringing things to the surface for the sake of it. We are not talking about an unhealthy and negative introspection. We are talking about allowing ourselves to be touched, healed, forgiven and transformed by the Spirit of God who wants to make us more like Christ.

## The foundation

Roger Hurding, in his excellent book *Restoring the Image*, identifies five foundational qualities of the good counsellor.

*(i) Experience of affliction.* The hard grind of experience is the best teacher.

*(ii) Empathy.* Not just pity but having an identity factor added, and the will to do something about the problem. Someone has said that, when a person falls into a ditch, apathy watches, sympathy jumps in too but ends up equally stranded, while empathy keeps one foot on the bank, puts one in the ditch and starts to pull them out.

*(iii) A good listener.* Often quoted, seldom noted!

*(iv) Non-judgemental.* Point righteous fingers and you've lost the case.

*(v) Persistence.* People are intricate personalities. They need time.

In Scripture it is clear that God's plan for people is that they grow and develop into the likeness of Christ. Our lives can get so cluttered with unnecessary additions, that we end up dragging heavy weights around rather than being released to be who God intended us to be. In the Revised Standard Version 2 Corinthians 3:18 says: 'And we all, with unveiled face, beholding the glory of the Lord, are being changed into his likeness from one degree of glory to another.'

Ephesians 4:11–16 says:

To build up the body of Christ ... come together to that oneness in our faith ... we shall become mature people, reaching to the very height of Christ's full stature. Then we shall no longer be children ... instead, by speaking the truth in a spirit of love ... the whole body grows and builds itself up through love.

## The framework

If we are going to help people, we must build a framework based on relationship, and not on a framework of operations.

### Step into

Young people need to know we care and are approachable. This will involve involvement! Stepping into situations with them. Not losing grip because of our unreality or misreading the situation, we must stand with them, learning to take in the scenery from their point of view. Don't step in uninvited, however. This is a privilege that is not automatic, but which must be earned. Never invade their space. Get their permission at each step of the helping procedure. Be aware of the crisis points when intervention may be needed: bereavement, job loss, unemployment, exam failure, broken relationships.

### Walk through

Pay attention. Listen carefully. If you are thinking of your answer all the time somebody is explaining something, you are probably not listening properly. As you listen to the person it will allow them to release their feelings and give you an opportunity to discern exactly what they are saying. Often the problem they come to you with is not the real problem at all. There is something deep seated in their lives that needs dealing with before the symptoms can be cured.

There are certain ways of exploring the listening mode that will help you keep on track. For instance, punctuate their response by reflecting back to them what they are saying. This helps to clarify in their mind what is going on, and will also act as a check for you to make sure you are understanding what is being said. In the interaction between you and the person you are trying to help, be careful not to make statements which will lead them up a dead-end street and leave no room for manoeuvre. Use what some have called 'door openers' that encourage further response. These could be in the form of questions or sentences that allow for further exploration.

Make sure you have adequate time and have in fact told the person exactly what time there is for the interview. Usually one hour is sufficient for a first meeting. Observe distress signals which may come from body movements or voice tones. Make sure you walk through the situation with them, without dictating to them. Do not be afraid to refer the person to somebody else if the situation demands it— they may need more specialist help.

## Stand back

We all like to feel wanted, but beware of an unhealthy dependency. If the person being counselled becomes possessive of the counsellor, problems arise. The counsellor is a catalyst in that he should stimulate the person being counselled towards greater personal growth. There are some people who cannot survive without a problem—that's the problem they have. These folk can be time-consuming and unproductive. If people do not receive and act upon the targets set during the interview, then you must be firm and insist that they need to do so before you can help them further.

## Follow on

Keep a bird's-eye view of the situation. Further input may be required as other needs come to the surface through the healing, restoring process. Pray regularly for the people you are counselling and make sure they are integrated with a caring group of people in the church.

There are certain styles and approaches to counselling

adopted by different people. *Directive* counselling is like a bulldozer! You have a problem, I have the answer. This is it. *Integrity or reality therapy* is like a transporter. You have a problem. Let me tell you what I did when I had the problem. *Non-directive counselling.* So you feel you have a problem—what makes you feel that way? The process of self-discovery and realization of the solution. Non-directive counselling is usually the most effective and lasting method, because people who discover things for themselves under the guidance of the counsellor, will have the satisfaction of achieving something for themselves and be spurred on to resolve the issue.

## The facts

Let's now take a look at some of the things going on inside us that affect the way we think, feel and react.

It is now generally recognized that the brain records every experience we have, including the emotions and feelings that went with those experiences. Through the function of the memory, we can relive past experiences while remaining in the present. The experiences recorded may be deep in our subconscious mind creating a negative impression or triggering a certain kind of response when a similar situation is encountered. The person concerned may not be aware that this is happening. Sometimes a memory can come flooding back because of an external prod. If there is an ongoing negative association, problems can arise by way of blockages and shut-downs in certain areas of the person's life.

Hurtful and damaging experiences can come from a variety of sources. They may be things that happen to us outside of our control: accidents of nature, illness, bereavement, other people acting insensitively. The hurt can also come as a result of sin which has not been dealt with or as a result of wrong choices being made. Guilt can lead to a sense of failure and introspection. People who live with unforgiveness of hurtful situations inflicted on them by others, tend to blame others for their lack of success in life. Once they have dealt with the forgiveness issue, and been forgiven themselves, they face the fear of proceeding in life without an excuse for failure or bad performance. People must be willing to assume responsibility for their own lives and not get trapped into the prison of making others pay the bill.

Nothing, however, is too terrible for the Lord to touch and deal with! We must learn how to minister the healing, love and forgiveness of God. We can only be effective in this as the Holy Spirit operates through us and touches the lives of others.

## The function

The point of all this is that we are into the business of making disciples. I'd like to finish off this chapter by dealing with two vital aspects of youth leadership and counselling. Pre-natal and post-natal spiritual activity.

Some time ago a survey was carried out which came up with the horrifying fact that 95% of church members in Great Britain have never led one person to Jesus Christ. Bringing people into the family of God by new birth is the business of the kingdom of God. The Holy Spirit makes it possible as he brings to life the dead dormant spirit inside the person, and he becomes whole.

How do you lead a person to Jesus? It's helpful to have some kind of outline in your mind that you can work with. This helps to give cohesion to what you are saying and helps you remember what you want to say. Evangelism Explosion is one method which I have used in a church to train people in evangelism. We found it to be highly effective because people were learning an outline gospel presentation upon which they would hang illustrations, personal observations and testimony. The danger in this kind of method is of course that it can become mechanical and unreal. This need not happen. The outline is there to help, not to tie down. So flexibility is again the key.

The facts that need to be explained to the enquirer are as follows:

(i) God's creation was perfect, but has been perverted by sin. Sin is rebellion against God. We have all sinned.

(ii) If you break a law you must pay the penalty. We have all broken God's law and the Bible clearly teaches that the 'wages of sin is death'. So we are all under a death sentence.

(iii) Because God loved us so much, he came in the person of Jesus Christ to do something we could never do for ourselves. He died on a cross to pay the penalty we deserved.

(iv) If we want to know God personally, we must repent, believe and receive God's gift of forgiveness and new life. Repentance is not merely saying 'sorry'. It is a complete reversal of life, turning around and following God's way. Being determined, with God's help, never to backtrack and make the same mistakes again.

(v) God will then come and live in us and empower us with his Holy Spirit, helping us to explore and move into the special place he has for us in his plan.

When talking to enquirers, be sure they understand. Use illustrations to help explain what you mean. You may know the story of the man standing in court being sentenced by the judge, amazed to see the judge come down and pay the penalty for the man. This is a perfect example of what Jesus did for us. There is a growing receptivity to the things of God in these days. We must take the opportunities and make them grow into new people joining the family of God. Ask enquirers to repeat a prayer of acceptance after you. Pray for them. Make sure they are linked to a good local fellowship who will support and care for them.

The first few hours and days are crucial for the new Christian. Be ready with nurture groups set up for the new Christians, maybe meeting in people's homes. Get the new converts linked quickly to a nurture group and also, at a more personal level, get them linked on a one-to-one basis with someone of the same sex and roughly the same age.

New Christians need to go through basic faith-building exercises and familiarize themselves with the tools for effective Christian living.

They need to know about how essential it is to read the Bible regularly for spiritual food and growth. Prayer is a regular 'must' as this builds relationship with God and keeps the hotline open for anything. Telling others is crucial as we exercise our spiritual muscles in a hostile environment. They need to join a good spiritually-based, Christ-centred church. It is vital to belong to the family of God and this involves commitment. They need to know about the power of the Holy Spirit and the command of Scripture that all men should be baptized. They need to know how the Holy Spirit gives gifts to the people of God, in order that the body of Christ, the church, might be edified and grow, and so that others will know that God is alive today. We must think of their future. How will they operate in the church? What involvements should we encourage?

They are entering into a brand new experience with a new set of priorities, a new outlook on life, new goals to reach. They need space, time, encouragement and help to survive.

God has given us the resources. All we need to do is obey.

# 6

## *A Rainbow over South Ashford*

In this chapter we are going to look at how a youth work can function in all kinds of church situations, bringing about a power-packed programme and growth potential both numerically and spiritually. As before, I want to earth what I say in real-life situations I have encountered, to take it out of the theoretical into the reachable.

As my four-year course at Spurgeon's Theological College was drawing to an end, I was looking around to find the kind of church situation that I would fit into. I visited several possibilities and then heard about a church on a council estate in a London overspill area in Kent. Before we even visited the place my wife, Sue, and I were convinced this was where God was leading. A few months later at the tender age of twenty-four I became the pastor of the Baptist church at South Ashford in Kent. On the day of my 'induction' a rainbow appeared over the church, which we took to be a remarkable confirmation that this was of God.

I have seen God at work in small churches on many occasions. In my teenage years my parents saw the rapid growth of a youth club started in their home and graduating to the local 'Tin Chapel' later to become Minster Road Baptist Church on the Isle of Sheppey. A lot of healthy foundations were laid in my life during that time. Now as the pastor of a church I was to learn, often the hard way, how to put the theory into practice.

As a clergyman I was involved with the usual 'hatchems, matchems and dispatchems', and very quickly learned how things worked. One of my first baptismal services was a memorable occasion. I had never baptized anyone by full immersion before, so on the afternoon before the big service I practised on a local vicar friend! When I stood in the pool with my first real-life 'candidate', I was so anxious about getting him under the water and up again that I was a little too enthusiastic in my actions. As the man hit the water, an almighty splash hit both the organist and the piano player on either side of the pool. Three at once...not bad going!

South Ashford holds dear memories for me. It was here that Sue gave birth to our two children, Rebecca and Sarah-Jane. Both were born on a Sunday. The church secretary stood in for me on each occasion!

I was the pastor for five years and learnt so much during that time. How to develop a consistency in preaching and teaching week after week. How to cope with pastoral problems of all shapes and sizes. How to relate to both old and young alike with their different needs and back-grounds. How to introduce new ideas for worship, fellow-ship and outreach. Not every battle was won. Some tensions remained unresolved. Yet God did remarkable things in that place and we praise him for it!

The numbers of young people attending grew rapidly from just a handful to forty, then fifty, then sixty. We started meeting in our home and when we couldn't fit anybody else in, we moved to the church hall. I believe we discovered a healthy pattern for growth.

An open youth club situation can provide a social facility for young people, but if you want to introduce them to Jesus, I have found the best way is to start with a few committed young people and get them to invite their friends to a creative programme where they will not be 'preached' at but rather be exposed to relevant truths that will touch their lives and connect with them in a way that is down to earth and personal.

In these early years I had no particular strategy for youth work—it was being formulated as we were exposed to different situations. The best way to learn! It's no good formulating a great strategy, spending hours coming up with snazzy programmes and scintillating events, creating administrative headaches for organizers and leaders, and then discovering that your great earth-shattering plans do not connect with the young people! That's like building a great canon to be used in warfare and then, when the big moment comes for it to be fired, a peanut drops out of the end! This is the great danger in youth work. We need to be people-centred rather than programme-centred. I'm not suggesting that we should not have fancy programmes! But let's make sure we are firmly locked in to where our young people are, rather than pouring a load of irrelevant ideas onto them in which they will merely drown.

## Take a cool look at your situation

Take the opportunity to get out of your situation for a few hours in order to obtain a bird's eye-view of where you have been, where you are and where you think you are going. What is working? What isn't? What leadership have you got? Where are the needs? Where is the potential? How do things fit into the life and work of the church generally? Is there adequate communication? Are you in touch with the Lord yourself or have you lost it? What are your own family life and relationships like?

This exercise could result in a massive rethink, restructure and rebuilding. It's healthy to evaluate honestly before God what is happening in our lives and our service for him. We can only be effectively operational when we allow the Spirit of God to touch our lives and effect changes as and when necessary. This will filter through to our 'on the ground' operations.

An experience like this happened to me in a big way while I was at this first church in Ashford. After one Sunday evening service I had just arrived back home, which wasn't too far as the house was next door to the church, when there was a knock on the door and there was a young man who claimed that the devil had hold of him and he was desperate for help. I was about to enter a situation that I could not handle! We sat in the kitchen opposite one another and he told me his story getting more and more agitated as he went along. He poured out a whole load of things that indicated he was hurting inside, but more than that, he was gripped by the activity of the enemy in a highly unsubtle way! The enemy was operating and proud of it!

At any moment I thought I might be floored by a flying right hook to the jaw, so I held on to his wrists tightly and spoke words, prayed, pleaded, panicked(!) and then discovered the wonder of the peace of the Spirit of God taking over. We were there together for a couple of hours, and when he left the situation had been transformed. It was the work of God.

I went up to my room and started to praise God and sing, 'From the rising of the sun to the going down of the same, the Lord's name is to be praised!' At that moment I opened my Bible and it fell open at Psalm 113. I had just been singing these very words. My tiredness from the day's ministry had gone. I had experienced God at work that night. I sensed the presence of God in my life in a way I had not done before. It was as if the Spirit of God had been locked away in my life and suddenly been released. I had been let loose on planet earth! From that moment I looked at things from a different perspective. God no longer seemed remote and unreachable. My ministry took on a new vitality.

It doesn't matter what 'label' you put on an experience like that. The big question is this: Are we operating in the power of the Holy Spirit? That's the fundamental question we all need to answer. If we are not, let's resolve this issue by surrendering again to the lordship of Jesus and all that this implies. If we are, let's move on!

## Build a framework

When we have had a time of evaluation before God and got our priorities right in terms of people first, programmes second, then we can construct a framework for operations in our situation that will enable us to grow.

After our small home meeting grew at South Ashford, we moved into the church building to allow for more growth, and at that point began to formulate a framework to cater for the growing numbers of young people attending. Since those five years working as pastor at South Ashford, I have moved into a variety of situations, some dramatic, some fairly normal; some earth shattering and others routine. After leaving South Ashford, I was itinerant as a musician/communicator for six years, during which time I discovered some amazing truths. More of that later. Later I was youth pastor at the Millmead Centre Baptist Church in Guildford as part of a pastoral team. I had a three-year projected plan of operations outlined during my first month of being at the church. This was it:

*Phase one*:   Spend the first year getting to know people, developing a youth leadership training course, and start a regular programme of outreach activities.

*Phase two*:   During the second year, with the help of the youth leaders, completely restructure the youth framework under a new theme title, introducing some new programme ideas and rethinking the old ones.

*Phase three*:   The third year I wanted to start a project using a double-decker bus and full-time voluntary team made up of young people in the church who were called to give a year out. Also to develop the idea of ministry teams, going out representing the church in 'on the job training' exercises. We also wanted to major in on caring for people and consolidating growth.

The framework for youth operations that emerged at Millmead was operating way back in the South Ashford era (although it was not as sophisticated or well thought out in those days). So I do believe that whatever size church you are involved with, this kind of framework can operate effectively and carries with it the ingredients essential for healthy growth. (See diagram.)

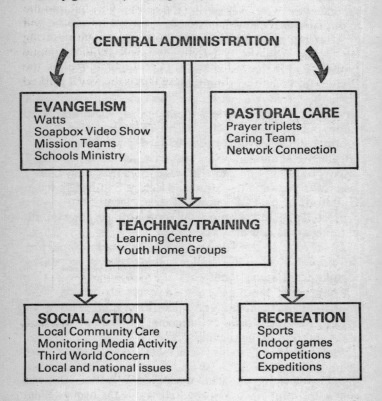

*Essential ingredients for youthwork*

We need to think about effective evangelism/communication; pastoral care/counselling; Bible-centred, life-related teaching; community care and social action; personal development and recreational facilities; administration. We're going to take a look at these six areas now and see how they work out in practice. I'm using the Millmead youth group structure as a model which is adaptable to fit into any situation. Don't, however, fall into the trap of thinking that the specific ideas we have used will work anywhere—it's the general principles I am referring to. Your situation is unique and will require unique handling. We chose the name 'The Light Force' as the theme title for our youth activites. This is the way it worked out:

## 1. Effective evangelism/communication

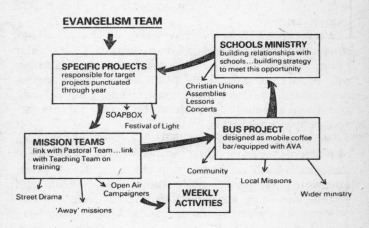

Our Friday night youth club was called 'WATTS'. This was the advertising blurb we used to describe the event: 'Want to air your views on vital issues like the nuclear debate, drug abuse, the Third World, sexual relationships, race relations? Want to meet your friends, have a cup of coffee and listen to music in a friendly atmosphere? Want opportunities to take part in creative workships like drama, dance, photography, video production, music, sculpture, mime? Want to get some training in soccer, rugby, basketball, table tennis? Want to get advice about your legal rights, family problems, life direction, kicking the drug habit, discovering your potential? WATTS is the new youth venue for Guildford. WATTS is the place where you can bring your friends. WATTS is the place where you will not be preached at. WATTS could be a revolutionary experience!'

I know what you are thinking! There is no way you feel you could provide those kinds of facilities in your situation. But think about it. What are the untapped resources in your area? What grants could you get from the local authority? What students are there near you who would love to do a workshop? What people in your church have hidden talents?

We see WATTS as the place where we channel all our contacts through our evangelism ministry. It's the regular Friday night slot when we encourage our young folk to mix with those coming for the first time and engage in one-to-one evangelism. There is no preach, no epilogue, but we do encourage a friendly atmosphere and a place that encourages people to find Jesus.

We also have regular 'specials'. We developed the idea of a video chat show called 'Soapbox'. Using a variety of ingredients such as drama, pop videos, dance, reviews, interviews, live music, crazy stunts, news bulletins and jingles, the show has been effective in being a highly contemporary form of communication and many have been helped through this. We have also used the more traditional 'rock concert' approach. We called our series 'The Rock Warehouse' and this was successful and fruitful.

One technical point. When using pop videos and music for public performance, make sure you first of all obtain a licence from the Publishing Rights Society and the necessary copyright clearance.

Part of our evangelism involves taking teams of young people out 'on mission'. We have been able to take teams to Germany and Holland, and this has given confidence and experience to folk out in the battle field. We have also been involved in street drama and door-to-door visitation. My own commitment to schools ministry has been expressed in contacts with many local schools on a regular basis, taking assemblies, lesson periods, concerts and Christian Unions. The approach to school work with its tremendous potential is dealt with in detail in another chapter, as is the whole area of how to communicate effectively.

## 2. Pastoral care/counselling

We have already said that to have an emphasis on pro-grammes is to be lopsided. We need the emphasis to be clearly on people. Young people need a lot of care and patience. With the unique pressures that they are facing and the changes that they are having to cope with physio-logically, we must spend adequate time and energy on the vital area of caring support. We are gradually developing a framework for this to be effective in our youth group. Things like prayer triplets, which encourage interaction on a regular basis, and a 'caring team' of people who will fulfil pastoral roles with groups of young people. We also experimented with something we called 'The Network Connection'. Everybody is identified on a grid, and is asked to keep contact with other folk around them on the grid. When the system works efficiently, it means that everybody feels part of the family.

Young people easily detect reality in relationships and will turn off when we come out with 'stock' answers that sound superspiritual but actually miss the target completely. R. E. O. White in his book *A Guide to Pastoral Care* says: 'Though we point men beyond ourselves to Christ, yet we will never take them further than we ourselves have come.'

We found that having someone with specific respon-

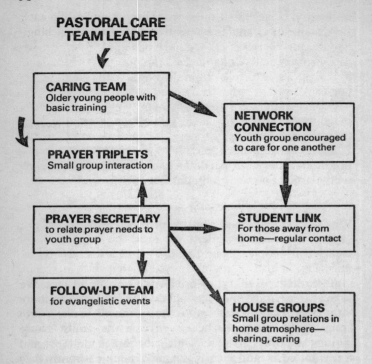

sibility to co-ordinate and control a pastoral care/counselling programme is vital for the growing youth group. This person will identify others with gifts in counselling and will encourage and train them in techniques and approaches that are effective.

I have dealt with caring/counselling in other chapters of this book. It must have a definite place in our framework for youth work, with a strategic plan of operations.

### 3. Bible-centred, life-related teaching

Someone once said, 'All word and no Spirit, you dry up; all Spirit and no word, you blow up; Word and Spirit you grow up.' The Holy Spirit brings the word of God alive to us and we need to be sure that the word is becoming flesh in each situation we face. That is the essence of life-related teaching.

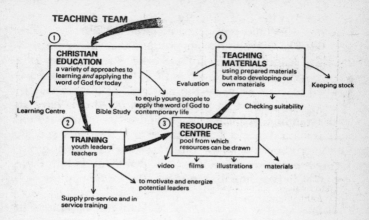

At Millmead we have a Learning Centre for all ages. We have two identical morning services, and in between there is the opportunity for life-related Bible study. In our Youth Learning Centre, we operate at two main levels. Those aged between eleven and fourteen come into JAM, and study a variety of themes relevant to them. Currently they are studying how being a Christian affects the way we look at things like boy/girl relationships, family life, telling others, prayer and Bible reading. The older fifteen-plus group is called 'Highlights' and operates using a series of 'customized' Bible studies which again are geared to relevant issues.

Teaching techniques need to be varied, creative and constructive. I would encourage participation, debate, simulation games, question and answer, activity work, drama and workshops as part of the teaching process. There are some good teaching resources available. The teaching aids we have used include: the 'Serendipity' series from the Bible Society; Gospel Light youth materials; our own customized studies using *Jam* magazine as a spring-board; the 'Life' and 'Growth' courses produced by the Christian Publicity Organisation and the 'Beginnings' series produced by the Bible Society.

When selecting appropriate material there are questions you need to ask about your group: What issues are they facing at school, college, home, work? Where are they at in their understanding of God? Is there a particular emphasis needed in your group at the moment? Is there a lack of understanding about a particular issue? Do they have an understanding of what's happening in the world around and how it relates to their situation? Do they need specific guidance about their own future? Is somebody in the group facing a life crisis that needs to be dealt with in the whole group (a bereavement, family break up, exam failure, job loss, etc.)?

It may be that you will need to adapt the material to fit your circumstances. There is nothing worse than laboriously ploughing through material that has no relevance to life. The teaching, learning process is vital for growth and can be fun if approached in a creative way.

## 4. *Community care and social action*

Looking inwards creates an unreality in church people that divorces what they do in church from the real world. Social action is coming back on the agenda after years of suspicion from good evangelicals who were afraid that we would preach a social gospel that declares salvation is brought about by doing good things. God is giving us back our sense of responsibility for the world in which we live, and caring for people and highlighting injustice has become a real opportunity to demonstrate the love of God, thus creating endless opportunities for evangelism.

We encourage our young people to take caring initiatives in our community—not with the ulterior motive of then being able to preach at people, but because we feel that it is part of what Jesus meant when he said we were salt and light in the world. There are different aspects to social action and each have their place.

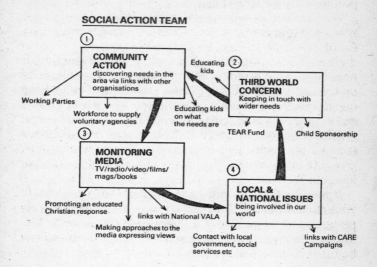

**SOCIAL ACTION TEAM**

① **COMMUNITY ACTION** discovering needs in the area via links with other organisations

Working Parties

Workforce to supply voluntary agencies

Educating kids

② **THIRD WORLD CONCERN** Keeping in touch with wider needs

Educating kids on what the needs are

TEAR Fund        Child Sponsorship

③ **MONITORING MEDIA** TV/radio/video/films/mags/books

Promoting an educated Christian response

links with National VALA

Making approaches to the media expressing views

④ **LOCAL & NATIONAL ISSUES** being involved in our world

Contact with local government, social services etc

links with CARE Campaigns

*(a) Local community care.* Do your homework before launching out. Carry out a survey in your area to find out what the needs are. There will be the obvious ones of unemployment, drug abuse, homelessness...but there may be other needs in your area that do not have a high profile and therefore do not attract adequate help. Mobilize your young people into groups and get them out into practical action. Make sure you have a contact with the social services. They will be able to identify needs for you and suggest ways in which you can be involved. When dealing with problems such as drug abuse, or seeking to help those living in 'squats', make sure you know what you are doing. There are people with expertise in these areas like the London City Mission who are involved in these kinds of situations every day.

*(b) Third World concern.* Getting a bigger view of the world and becoming involved in practical action will expand the love and understanding of your group. This is a vital element in opening new areas of commitment and concern. It also puts into perspective the materialistic attitude of the community in which we live and encourages the young people radically to consider a change of lifestyle.

Sponsoring a child through one of the relief agencies like Tear Fund or World Vision will provide personal interest in a Third World project. These organizations also have excellent ideas for youth group involvement and action. Christian Aid have an excellent simulation activity called 'The Trading Game' which is fun to do but carries a lot of clout in terms of being an eye opener to the real world.

*(c) Monitoring media activity.* Another dimension to social action and community care, is having an informed and active role in monitoring the media. Having met Mary Whitehouse personally when she appeared as a guest on our Soapbox Video Show, it highlighted for me again how isolated and misunderstood someone can become when they are tackling the crucial issues of our TV diet. The time has long gone when we Christians can get by unnoticed by the world. It's time to make a stand. There are more people on our side than you imagine, but because of the highly vocal minority, we are subjected to explicit scenes of sex and violence that are feeding twisted minds and turning fantasy into reality on our streets.

When Mary Whitehouse was interviewed on the TV news programme *Newsnight*, she was drawing attention to the horrific scenes that formed part of a season of films shown on Channel 4. A spokesman for the TV channel, trying to defend the showing of these films, explained that they had developed the idea of having a Red Triangle sign on the screen so that people were warned in advance that there might be scenes which would be offensive. It's not surprising that she replied that the films were watched by twice as many people than would normally watch Channel

4 films. The Red Triangle seems to be a great advertising gimmick. She went on to say that adults ought not to be left to make adult decisions about what they should and shouldn't watch. Adults make 'adult decisions' about of lot of things...planting bombs in cars, raping innocent women, mugging old people in their homes and abusing children.

Producers of TV programmes take notice of public opinion. Next time, don't just switch off and pretend it didn't happen. Let's have our say. Write letters of encouragement when you see something good, but don't hesitate to speak out when things are wrong.

*(d) Speaking into local and national issues.* CARE Campaigns, based in London, are doing a great job in bringing to the surface issues which we ought to be concerned about as Christians. The Evangelical Alliance is also involved in representing a large proportion of the church in England and has a variety of materials available that can help educate and motivate a youth group into action on national issues.

One year we decided that on Halloween we would have a Festival of Light. Around 200 young people marched through the town with banners and torches declaring clearly that the kingdom of light is more powerful than the kingdom of darkness. We gave out leaflets and invited people back to a Celebration in our church.

Community care and social action constitute one of the ways we can apply the victory and see the enemy's strongholds come down.

## 5. *Personal development and recreational facilities*

In our concern to be 'spiritual' we often overlook the spiritual dimension of physical activity. God is concerned for our whole being and therefore we should make available to our young people opportunities for recreation. At our youth club we try to combine the activities of workshops, debates, which we call 'Bite the Bullet!', and recreation. We have football training, basketball, table tennis, snooker and pool. We also programme into our schedule visits to the bowling alley and ice-skating rink. The local council will often help financially with equipment if it can be shown that the club is for the benefit of the community.

Competitions, tournaments, races and games can be a good source of physical activity and often during these times real friendships can be made and strengthened. I'll never forget being invited to speak on a youth camp made up of mostly hostile young people out to put the boot in to the guest speaker! I was finding it hard to break through in the sessions, because of the general chaos around me! The stink bombs didn't help either! On the second afternoon of the week we all went off to an adult recreational park. I like doing crazy things at times. Some would say I have suicidal tendencies, but it's a lot of fun really. Through having a great time together, the ice was broken and we were able to communicate with those young people.

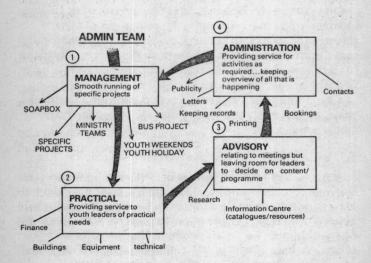

**ADMIN TEAM**

① **MANAGEMENT** Smooth running of specific projects

SOAPBOX

SPECIFIC PROJECTS

MINISTRY TEAMS

BUS PROJECT

YOUTH WEEKENDS YOUTH HOLIDAY

④ **ADMINISTRATION** Providing service for activities as required...keeping overview of all that is happening

Publicity

Letters

Keeping records

Printing

Contacts

Bookings

③ **ADVISORY** relating to meetings but leaving room for leaders to decide on content/ programme

Research

Information Centre (catalogues/resources)

② **PRACTICAL** Providing service to youth leaders of practical needs

Finance

Buildings Equipment technical

## 6. Administration

I have found it is best to have a central administration. In other words, one person who carries the can! Work can be delegated to appropriate people, but it needs central co-ordination. Administration will be responsible for things like:

*Finance*: Keep accurate records of all transactions and be ready to submit the accounts for auditing before the end of each financial year. Try to work out a budget twelve months in advance so that financial targets can be set and prayer begun!

*Publicity and promotion*: Shoddy artwork will not do! Let's get professional in our approach and design good quality artwork and graphics with personalized logos for our youth work. This logo should appear on everything that goes out so that the group begins to build an identity and image in the area. Make contacts with the local news-papers, radio and TV stations and make sure they receive regular press releases about the things you are doing. The Christian Publicity Organisation in Worthing have some excellent samples of promotional literature.

*Organizing events*: A concert presentation needs to be organized well in advance and the publicity ready to go out three months before the event. Make sure people are avail-able on the night for things like stewarding, counselling, catering, and bouncing(!). Make sure also that you have a systematic and organized approach to follow-up.

*Home base activities*: Central administration should also take care of room booking for youth events, and use and care of equipment.

*Church links*: There must also be a communications procedure so that news reaches the family of the church to which you are linked. Prayer and practical support will come from the church family when proper links are maintained.

*Keeping records*: A card index system is essential. Contact your folk at crucial times like birthdays, anniversaries, school exam results, bereavements.

*Regular youth leaders' meetings*: Essential for you to meet at least once a month for prayer and sharing times. Have a projected plan of action for twelve months at a time. Make sure your programme is organized in detail three months in advance. And get the whole thing bathed thoroughly in prayer.

## The beginning!

We have looked at a framework which I believe can work anywhere. Whether it's a South Ashford Baptist Church in a London overspill area, or a Millmead Centre in the so-called Bible belt. Our objectives are to win young people for Christ; to make them disciples of Jesus; to build them into the family of God; and to help them express that relationship in every area of life. We must model before our young people what we are preaching at them. This is where we begin! Check out what God is saying to you. Evaluate your clientele. Get input from young people you are already connected with. Be locked in firmly to the local church. Stand back and watch the Spirit move!

# 7

## *I Believe in Aeroplanes*

### Emergency regulations!

'Ladies and gentlemen. Welcome to flight 101. We would like to assure you of our best attention at all times during this flight. We will be travelling at 37,000 feet and expect to arrive at our destination in about seven hours from now. May I draw your attention to the safety regulations. This is the world's safest passenger airline. If, however, we get into difficulties there is a life jacket underneath your seat which fits like this.... There is also an oxygen mask that will come down from the ceiling if we lose air pressure. Place this over your nose and mouth and breathe normally. You will have a really nice feeling as we go down. There are five exit doors on this side of the aircraft and five on that side. If we land in the sea, plastic shutes will open up and you can slide down these into the sea. The kids really love it! There will be a choice of three meals during the flight. (There is a plastic bag in the pocket of the seat in front of you.) We also have in-flight entertainment. Our special film for this trip is *Airport 87*. Now fasten your safety belts and there is to be no smoking on take-off and landing. Have a nice trip!'

If you were worried about flying before, now you are paranoid!

This description illustrates a basic spiritual truth that

many of us still have not grasped. There is a difference between believing and trusting. I can believe in aeroplanes. I can study the law of aerodynamics. I can collect pictures of aircraft and stick them on the wall. I can use binoculars and identify aircraft in the sky. But it's only when I go up in one that I have 'completed' my belief by personal experience. I trust in the things that I believe with my mind, and I take physical risks as I allow my belief to be tested by the cut and thrust of live action. If there is one thread running right through this book, this is it!

A new chapter of my life began with one of the greatest challenges to my Christian faith I have experienced so far. I had been prepared to talk about faith, preach about it, pray about it, sing about it . . . was I now prepared to prove it! It's easy to believe the text hanging on the wall: 'My God will supply all your needs according to his riches in glory in Christ Jesus.' Now I was to discover its truth.

### Prepare for take-off

After five years as pastor of the Baptist church in South Ashford, God opened up a totally unexpected door for us into a specialized ministry communicating with young people. The next six years saw me travelling to many parts of the world, appearing on television, performing on radio and recording LPs. Using contemporary music and creative communication, I worked in a variety of settings from Wembley Arena to Wandsworth Prison; school classrooms to mainstage Greenbelt; seedy bars to the streets of San Francisco!

I had given in my notice at the church in South Ashford on the strength of an invitation we had received from a church in London to become their youth pastor. I would work in the church for a certain amount of the year and be released to travel for the rest. That seemed like a great idea. We prepared for the move believing that this was really from the Lord. Just a short time before we were due to move, the church reversed what had seemed to be a concrete decision and we were left high and dry. I could not go back, as my notice had been given. So we put our furniture in store: some of it went into a minister friend's loft, some went into another friend's garage and other bits and pieces were spread around! Sue and I, with our two children Rebecca and Sarah-Jane, got into our car and headed for Cornwall. That was the first miracle. We had the use of a cottage on the north coast of Cornwall for a month at the peak of the holiday season. It just happened to be available to us....

During those weeks God began to get us into shape for an exciting, demanding, rewarding, tiring ministry! I did a few concerts in the area and gradually the engagements came in. Without any advertising or pushing, the work opportunities came in from all over the place, including opportunities to work in Europe, America and Asia. We had no set income or permanent accommodation, but we discovered the 'text' was true. We had our struggles, temptations, doubts and fears, but we knew all along it was God who built the ministry and who supplied the needs.

You may be at the point in your life when you are wondering what God has in store for the future. Whether you are a young person getting ready to take off into an as yet unknown destination, or whether you feel God is indicating a change of direction in your life, you may be considering right now what the next step is. Nothing is ever as easy and straightforward as the booklets make out, and there is always a danger of confining the ways of God into neat formulas, but there are some general principles that are crucial to observe when we are looking for God to point the way forward. As I was launching out into a new area of ministry, these are the pointers that helped me.

## Purposefully commit your way to the Lord

Psalm 37:5 puts it like this: 'Give yourself to the Lord; trust in him and he will help you.' The well-known, much-quoted verses in Proverbs 3:5–6, also apply: 'Trust in the Lord with all your heart and lean not on your own understanding; in all your ways acknowledge him, and he will make your paths straight' (New International Version). Of course, it's easy to quote verses and have a high resolve to be 'sold out' for God, but what does it really mean? We've all heard countless sermons on the importance of Jesus being Lord of our lives and putting him in the number one position on our list of priorities. We've all struggled with the genuine desire to put Jesus on the throne of our lives, but feeling that we somehow never quite get there. On the other hand, if we say we have got there, we feel this is a slightly unspiritual thing to say because in the back of our minds there is the thought that actually you are never really meant to get there until you reach glory.

The problem with all of this, of course, is that we get trapped in a 'no man's land'; a kind of self-annihilation programme that seems vaguely spiritual, but results in us never passing first post in our search for the will of God for our lives. Thank God he is much more 'human' than we sometimes imagine! God knows what it's like to struggle with the problems of being human.

We've been talking a lot about closing the credibility gap (demonstrating God to the world) and closing the communication gap (learning how to connect with people where they are). However, the biggest single barrier to preventing this from happening is the gap we ourselves have created between us and God. The problem is everywhere in the Christian church. Young people and older people living their Christian lives in a kind of resigned pessimism. We believe God is there, but he too often seems a million miles away from us.

One of my most memorable love affairs took place when I was nine years of age! Jean Springate was the most beautiful girl I had ever seen! I used to follow her home from school and stand outside the flat where she lived looking up at the window. She lived above a row of shops in

Norwood High Street in London, and it was difficult to work out exactly which was the right window to look at. Undaunted, I would look from a distance at the girl of my dreams. At my junior school we had a tradition faithfully adhered to every year. All the pupils would line up and collect a daffodil bulb each. We had to take them home and nurture them and come back with our fully-grown daffodil in the spring. The best one received a special prize. I never did receive a prize, but I did have the aim to present this flower in all its glory to Jean. This became such a big thing in my life that I even dreamt about it!

There was Jean Springate coming out of school one day when suddenly she was violently attacked by 100 giant daffodils! I went to the rescue and with a giant pair of scissors, chopped off all the heads of the daffodils saving Jean from a fate worse than death!

The 'relationship' went on for twelve months, but the tragedy of the story is that never once did I speak personally to her! I wrote notes to her which were passed round the classroom, followed her home from a distance every day, looked admiringly up at her window...but never spoke to her.

That's the tragedy which has invaded the church also! We have adopted a second-hand faith living on the backs of those we perceive as being 'spiritual'. We build our relationship with God on the experiences of others rather than on a real personal encounter with God. So many feel, at best, that this is the norm for the Christian life and at worst that God has abandoned them!

If we are going to commit our way purposefully to the Lord, we need a new relationship with him based on a personal encounter.

Some of the reasons for this distanced relationship with God are hinted at right there in Proverbs 3:5–6.

*When our heart is somewhere else*

Jesus said, 'Where your treasure is, there will your heart be also.' Living on our past experiences or having self-centred priorities merely creates barriers to the flow of the relationship God wants with you. Make a list of the priorities that you feel God has for his people and then make a list of your personal priorities in order of importance. How do the two compare? How do you rectify the situation? By an act of the will. You have to decide to get it right. With that resolve and a lot of help from the Spirit, you can rearrange your life and get back on track with God.

### When we lean on our own understanding

I've lost count of the number of times I have sat in my van seething because I've encountered yet another traffic jam in the heart of London. It seems unavoidable these days, yet I'm sure with a better knowledge of the A to Z map of London, I could find easier routes through the city. The radio station helicopter circles overhead giving traffic reports. It must be great to have a bird's eye view of the situation.

We will only survive in our walk with God when we cultivate a relationship with him that puts us in touch with his view of things. When we experience things in our lives that we find hard to handle, or when questions are posed that seem to have no answer, or when we watch other situations that don't seem to fit our view of a loving God in action...it is only when we can see earthly things from a heavenly point of view that we can survive and grow. If we always take the practical, predictable cerebral route in our Christianity, it will lead us into spiritual suicide.

Of course it is right to have a well thought out, reasoned faith. I'm not knocking an intellectual approach, but we create the 'gap' when we fail to get beyond our reasoned arguments. We can purposefully commit our way to the Lord when we have thought through the options, measured our lives up against the greatness of our God and then by an act of the will, decided to give all to him, whatever the cost.

## Prayerfully seek his will for your life

If our relationship with God becomes theoretical, it's prayer that goes first. We tend to fly blind by relying on guess work in the hazy hit-and-miss world of life that has lost the glow. We have to deal with this if we are going to get back on course with God. Prayer is the vital link in communicating with God and is a two-way thing. Talking and listening are all part of this discovery process and are things that need to be practised and perfected.

Past experiences can condition how we will react to present circumstances. I remember going back to Spurgeon's College several years after I had completed my theological course there and reliving experiences and emotions that I had felt all those years before. I stood in the chapel and could feel what it was like when I took part in my first sermon class. At least twice in the college course we had to prepare and present a service in front of the students and faculty. It was a nerve racking experience preaching to sixty hungry students and top class theologians, all with their note books at the ready! We even had a video camera recording every nervous twitch! Afterwards the prognosis began in the lecture hall where a lot of lessons were learned!

As I looked into the empty chapel on my return visit, all the old emotions came rushing back. I could even remember the sermon I preached. It was from Revelation and entitled 'The Three Doors'. I remember the sense of elation I felt when the college principal, at that time Dr George Beasley Murray, said afterwards that he had not noticed the connection between the three doors before: the open door of opportunity (Revelation 3:8, the closed door of the church (Revelation 3:20) and the open door of vision (Revelation 4:1).

There are sometimes negative experiences that can create blockages in the way we view things. Trying to choose a name for my third child was coloured by certain criteria. There are some names that I identify immediately with people I have met in the past who have not left a good impression on me. So the name becomes a synonym of the attitude I have towards that person.

If we are going to seek prayerfully the Lord's will for our lives, it must be on the basis of something new. A new attitude, a new expectation, a new anticipation of what God is going to do. If we approach him looking through the view finder of old experiences, our attitude can easily be affected and a blockage created.

God said through Isaiah the prophet: 'Do not cling to events of the past...watch for the new thing I am going to do' (Isaiah 43:18–19).

It is as we refer everything to God in prayer that we begin to develop a spiritual sense about the picture that God is putting together in our lives. There is nothing more exciting than to recognize the hand of God at work in situations and circumstances of life, directing and moving and running through the special and unique strategy he has for each individual life.

## Move positively in the direction given

Through the changing circumstances in my own life, as my ministry changed and the securities that I had relied upon were taken away, three issues were being worked out. First, faith is not just something you preach about! Second, the 'one man ministry' is a thing of the past. God is calling us as the body of Christ to exercise the gifts he has given in a responsible way. You cannot be a jack of all trades. God hasn't designed us to operate that way in his kingdom. Thirdly, if the 'established' church does not deliver the goods, should you drop out? The answer for me was 'No'. You don't change things by dropping out. You have more clout as you get involved. So I was determined to stay within the established church set up, retaining my credibility as a recognized 'clergyman' and trying from within that framework to break new ground for the kingdom.

One of the leaders within our Baptist denomination said I would be a 'pioneer', but pioneers have to 'pay the price'. We must not be so presumptuous as to imagine that we who think we are more enlightened have all the answers! We have much to learn from those who have been at the front line for many years. But as we take the strain and shoulder more of the responsiblity for our generation, we must hear what the Spirit is saying to the church in these days. We must move positively in the direction God gives, going for the open doors of opportunity.

You may be a young person reading this book desperately wanting to know where you are heading in the future. The principles outlined will help if you prayerfully apply them to your situation.

It could be you are a youth leader searching for new ideas and vision for the future. The same principles apply as you seek the Lord's direction for the vital role of ministry you are in.

If you are a parent, trying to understand your children, the same principles apply.

## Learning how to fly

Over the six years that I was in an itinerant ministry, we lived in empty Baptist manses. When the church found a minister it was time for us to move on! We lived for two years in each place. First Brighton, then Rainham in Kent, then Orpington. Each time God provided loving, caring people for us to relate to and join with, although we could never quite get over the 'temporary' feeling of knowing we could not really settle. The one constant factor was our life together as a family and the work that God had called us to. Our family became 'extended' as we invited two single girls, whom we had known for some time, to become part of our life. Sue and Jeanette were to be with us for several years, and this brought a deep friendship and commitment into our lives together. We had others living with us for

shorter periods of time. Alison came and also James and
Richard who worked with me full time on the road, taking
responsibility for the technical and visual effects that had
become a trademark in our presentations.

As we purposefully commit our way to the Lord, prayerfully seek his will for our lives and positively move in the
direction given, we will find ourselves in the process of
learning how to fly!

## Automatic pilot

During those six years there was always a real sense that
God was developing a ministry and I was simply moving
through the open doors. I never did any massive advertising
campaigns or relied on 'high profile' gigs like Greenbelt,
the gigantic Christian arts festival that takes place over
August bank holiday (although I did appear on the coveted
mainstage one year!). Yet I was continually busy with
exciting opportunities to perform, preach and teach in
many situations all over the world. I also had opportunities
to be involved in television work, appearing as one of the
presenters of the long running and much acclaimed TVS
programme *Company* for two years. With other TV
appearances and a host of 'grass roots' opportunities, life
was full and adventurous! The best thing was that God
moved powerfully through my frailty.

As a fan of *Star Trek*, I love watching repeats of the
popular movie versions of the series. *The Search for Spock*
contained some great phrases and dramatic moments—
most of which were very predictable, yet because of their
predictability gave a feeling of warmth, security and familiarity to the plot and characters. Captain Kirk, watching his
Starship Enterprise crash into flames on a deserted planet
proclaims in despair, 'O Bones, what have I done!' Bones
(the medic on the crew) answers, 'What you had to do.
What you always do...turn death into a fighting chance to
live!' Brilliant!

Then there was the fantasy film, *Flash Gordon*, with the inevitable beautiful girl saying blissfully, 'O Flash, I love you, but we only have twelve hours to save the earth!' All good stuff! But....

Often the reason why we never get airborne spiritually, is that we have found our security in the predictable, safe surroundings of our pseudo-Christianity. We must take our hands off the controls and let the Spirit of God take us into automatic pilot. All the manoeuvring in the world never saved a lost soul or created a framework for Holy Spirit power operations. Automatic pilot means risky living. It means we must go where we are taken. But it means our lives enter a new dimension of reality and take off into undreamt of spiritual encounters which not only transform the participants but also the environment in which they live.

## Aiming high!

It is God's design for his people to hit the big time! I'm not talking about superstardom, although that may be his purpose for some. I'm talking about big people demonstrating the existence of a big God! For too long we have allowed ourselves to be pushed into corners of inconsistency, compromise and fear, because we have lost our confidence in the greatness of God. The call today from the Lord, is for his church to make its presence felt not by conventional predictable routines, but by supernatural God-given power!

Therefore we must learn how to think big. 'Give me this mountain!' said eighty-five-year-old Caleb when he was facing the most terrifying battle of his life.

Others have faced giants but trusted in the superior power of God to effect the victory. Aim high! Walk tall! In our personal lives, our relationships with others, our family life and in our work for the Lord, let's go for the big time and trust him for the resources.

Why did it take a Bob Geldof to think of Band Aid when

the church should have taken the initiative in the first place? When will we wake up to the fact that we are the answer to the problem and the problem is put in its right perspective when measured against the greatness, majesty, love and grace of our God.

# 8

## 'Is that Your Real Name, Sir?'

The Youth For Christ outfit in the area that I was due to work in got in touch with the local secondary school and asked if I could do a lunchtime concert while I was in the area. Strangely enough, the date they requested happened to be April Fool's Day. When the headmaster received the letter he assumed that he was being set up by one of the pupils. The facts he had were that my name was Flashman, I was a rock singer and an ordained clergyman! He could be forgiven for getting the wrong end of the stick! So in retaliation to what he thought was a prank, he designed some posters illustrating the 'rocking Rev.' in an amusing and slightly compromised way, and stuck them around the school. When I arrived on the day ready to perform you should have seen the look on the headmaster's face. I heard later that he hurriedly sent one of the sixth formers around the school to collect the posters before I saw them!

For many years the whole area of school missions has excited me and frustrated me at the same time. It's excited me because of the tremendous opportunities there are in schools and colleges around the country for Christians to go in and take assemblies, lesson periods, lunchtime events and Christian Unions. It's frustrated me because of the low profile school ministry has and the ignorance of so many to the possibilities.

So many in the field of music have been screaming out for years about the danger of the Christian music ghetto and of only performing to the small world of the Christian concert circuit. Schools work has been overlooked and ignored because it doesn't give you a very good image if you're a musician working in a schools ministry. You get patronizing write ups in the Christian press about the 'good work' being done, but you get the feeling that this area of work is really not for the professionals.

However, let's face it: you can't get more 'secular' than a comprehensive school assembly. Where else can you reach a non-Christian audience of thousands on a regular basis in live performances? Very few 'secular' bands get the opportunity of playing to numbers like that, yet here we have the opportunity of reaching the singles-buying public. But before we get all the record companies pushing their artists into the school circuit to make money, let's clear a few things up! It's not too difficult to get into a school to perform . . . but it's easy to mess things up and close the door on any further entrance into the school. It's not too difficult to get opportunities to operate in assemblies and lunchtime events . . . but there are rules which must be adhered to if the operation is going to be successful. That's what this chapter is all about.

First of all I'd like to take a bird's eye view of the education system to help us get a picture of what is happening at the moment, and then I'd like to take a deeper look at how you can get involved.


## EDUCATION UNDER PRESSURE

There is a general feeling of instability in our educational system in Britain, which has been growing over the years for a variety of reasons. Problems with wage agreements, working conditions, clarifying the role of the teacher, expectations placed upon the teacher outside of what ought to be expected, changing ideas on the exam/assessment systems, lack of finance for the ever-expanding needs that arise...these and other problems have occupied the thinking, energy and time of parents, pupils and teachers alike. Many feel we are not adequately educating our children to face the demands of the future and life in the next century. Education acts, green papers, white papers, exam papers, evaluations, recommendations and reports have left the system in a turmoil.

## Pressures on parents

We want the best for our children and we want them to receive a good all-round education that will help them to develop the equipment they need to contribute to society and live a fulfilled life. The pressure is on parents, however, in a variety of ways. Decisions have to be made that will affect the shape of things to come for our children. Many parents opt for a private education and that often means economic hardships and the ensuing family pressures. Those that could never afford that kind of education for their children have the right to choose where they receive their schooling, and this can often be governed by geographical considerations. One of the most important issues, however, is parents' involvement in their child's education.

As Christian parents we have a responsibility to be involved in this way. Do you know that the 1986 Education Act provides the opportunity for parents to be involved in decision-making on issues like sex education in your school? School governors have statutory powers to determine what form the sex education of a school shall be. Who will those governors be? Nominations can come from any area—local lesbian and gay groups; contraceptive manufacturers.... So what about the local Christian community? Most schools have a Parent/Teacher Association and it is good to foster links with the school in this way.

If you are unhappy with an aspect of your child's education, don't be afraid to see the head teacher about this. If it's on the question of sex education there could be ulterior motives behind the teaching approach. For instance, sometimes outside organizations are asked to be involved in the syllabus and they may have a particular emphasis in their presentation. Perhaps they are involved with the sale of contraceptives or the promotion of homosexual activities. Be sure. Find out. Get involved.

Don't let us forget that education is a joint affair. As parents we must share the burden. Children spend more time out of the home environment and under the influence of their teachers. This underlines the fact that we must get involved.

## Pressures on pupils

### (a) To believe

It may be pressure to believe in the kind of humanistic philosophy that says man's chief end is to glorify himself. It may be the kind that says we are all here by chance so must make the best of it; or the kind that says we must contribute and play our part in the ordering of society; or even a religious emphasis with the 'good works' angle attached. It may be helpful to emphasize the helping of others in our community—a lot of good projects have been undertaken—but there is still a 'cul-de-sac' feeling of, 'Where do we go from here?' in all of these approaches. The ultimate realities of life and the spiritual dimension are the missing links we must include.

Unfortunately when there is a 'religious' emphasis, say in a private school or a church-related establishment, it is often so high it is unreachable and totally irrelevant. At one school I worked in, these comments from pupils about chapel were typical: 'It's a half hour in the evening when I think of my maths'; 'It's all about stained glass, gold and pomp—doesn't make sense'; 'Christianity is normal people doing normal things—why dress up?'; 'We have people like sentries on the way to the chapel to make sure there is silence'; 'We have to sit there with our eyes closed and if we don't, we get jumped on afterwards with questions like, "Why weren't you being religious?"'

The 1944 Education Act states that there must be a daily assembly, a corporate act of worship. But the school assembly slot can be more of a joke than a genuine encounter with God, and simply reinforces the idea that 'religion' is boring and is to be avoided. I remember those boring irrelevant hymns about 'hobgoblins' and 'foul fiends' that seemed to belong to the realm of a childish attempt at a fantasy horror movie than an expression of Christian truth. The authoritarian approach of, 'You *will* enjoy this assembly!' has been an all-to-common feature in our schools, betraying the vote of 'no confidence' the teaching staff have to what they see as an unnecessary chore. Compulsory religious education in schools could be the very thing that will kill off the opportunity for something spiritually dynamic to happen in the lives of our young people.

### (b) To achieve

Many of the pupils who come from middle-class areas are under constant pressure from their parents and from the school to get good exam results. It looks good when compiling the annual report to have a good rate of success in examinations, and it gives parents something worth talking about with their neighbours! This can have a psychologically damaging effect on the young people and lead to all kinds of insecurities and negative responses in later life. I have talked to hundreds of pupils in secondary schools around the country who feel under pressure in this area and come out with things like: 'You're expected to be a good Christian science swot!'; 'When you're drunk it's good fun!'; 'Our life is run by bells'; 'The labels on your clothes *do* matter';

'People think we are so civilized that we only shop in Hobbs, Next, Jigsaw and French Connexion!' You can tell which quote comes from a private school!

The pressure to achieve is not necessarily focused on academics—it could be on physical prowess. In order to be accepted you have to be the best, bravest, fastest, fittest and strongest of the bunch. The competitive spirit can be a good and positive emphasis to encourage, but too often it can have overtones of success or failure measured by performance rather than encouraging people to reach their full potential as human beings.

After nearly two decades of debate, the former Education Secretary Sir Keith Joseph initiated a programme to amalgamate the GCE and the CSE into the new General Certificate of Secondary Education (GCSE). This has had a mixed reception from teaching staff and pupils alike, but in the main seems to be settling down to a positive pattern. However, it's encouraging that some schools are going beyond the exam results in terms of wanting to record the abilities and achievements of their children, recognizing that a piece of paper with grades on for eleven years of compulsory education is not a very satisfactory assessment. 'Profiles' or 'Record of Achievement' papers are given to show a continuous assessment of the young person's progress in a variety of ways and not just in academic abilities. The obvious problem with this approach is of course that, rather than a character assessment, some may end up with a character assassination.

### (c) To retrieve

The pressure is on to bring back into focus from the memory banks information which may have been deemed to be unusable in the modern world. The secondary school curriculum has often had an 'off switch' unintentionally programmed into the schedule because pupils have seen certain topics as irrelevant. They become bored, disillusioned and disruptive, some not even bothering to turn up for school.

The world is changing fast. There is still a real difficulty for many to obtain a job that will be fulfilling, so there is a lack of morale and purpose, especially among low-achieving children. The nature of work is changing too. Manufacturing industry has been in decline with traditionally skilled employment disappearing. Jobs in areas of high technology are on the increase, so high level skills, computer technology and science subjects seem in many cases, more appropriate. Then there can be an overweight of emphasis on learning facts and theories rather than the more practical life-related topics including creative and social skills.

We need to grapple with these issues in our education programmes if we are to be successful in providing a sound foundation for the future of our nation.

## Pressures on teachers

### (a) To economize

The number of children in secondary schools reached a peak in 1979, but there has been a steady decline in numbers which will reach the bottom of the curve in the 1990s. This is causing a massive reorganization in the system which has effectively closed many primary and secondary schools. The knock-on effect of this is that there are staff problems where schools are trying to cater for a wide variety of subjects on the curriculum. In some cases there may be only ten pupils taking a GCSE course, which means that someone has to decide on the viability of such a course. If it means taking on extra staff, that could be expensive and prohibitive when money is short.

Education is by far the most expensive service that the local authority has had to provide. It can often be up to 60% or 70% of the budget. There are over 100 local education authorities in this country and all are under pressure to economize.

## (b)  To compromise

With less money available there has been a real temptation
to cut corners and operate at a lower level in terms of
standards. If teachers feel the pressure of lack of facilities,
resources and remuneration, there can be a tendency to
view their occupation as merely a job rather than as a
vocation. During the latest political campaign to decide the
present government, education was high on the agenda of
all the parties, reflecting the real concern people have for a
new emphasis in educational standards backed up by adequate resources. Teachers need to know they have a crucial
role to play and that what they do must never be seen
merely as a job, but a vital contribution to the future of our
nation.

## (c)  To neutralize

Issues facing young people today, like the often tragic
consequences of sex before marriage, the abortion debate,
parental control, racial discrimination, the nuclear threat,
political issues, religious ideas, homosexuality...are all
taught from a neutral point of view. The pressure is on not
to make statements or to come out on one side of an issue.
The pupils must make their own judgements. The problem
is, you make judgements based on the facts presented and
these facts can often be incomplete or inadequate. In the
attempt to be neutral we have tried to give the facts for
inspection, but have fallen into the trap of becoming impersonal, mechanical and clinical in our approach, and
education is definitely not merely an intellectual exercise.

The devastating effects of the policy of some London
councils to teach that homosexual relationships are as OK
as heterosexual, will filter through into family life and
interpersonal relationships and create confusion and crisis
in the lives of many. It is dangerous and naive to develop
this policy. Maybe this is taught through plain ignorance of
those in authority as to the way children develop through a
natural phase of responding more to their own sex. But if

false information is injected at that crucial stage in the guise of wanting 'freedom of choice for all', then the developmental process can be diverted, perverted or stopped altogether.

Much has been made in the press about the racialist issue being blown out of all proportion with rules like, 'You must not order "black" coffee any more, but rather "coffee without milk".' The banning of 'Ba Ba Black Sheep' in certain schools, replacing it with 'Ba Ba Green Sheep', is hard to take seriously! However exaggerated the stories, the pressures are there to neutralize crucial issues for fear of offending people. The actual result, however, has often been to give an issue a profile out of proportion to its significance and create more problems than there were before.

### (d) To depersonalize

Leading on from the last section, the trend in the main has been a policy of little or no personal involvement with the pupils. The seemingly underrated position of teachers in our society has prompted a response of cold, conditional, functional relationships which are a means to an end and nothing else. I know for a fact that children and young people learn best in a relational atmosphere of mutual respect and caring concern. There has been a growing need for school counselling systems to be developed and many schools have highly effective ways of relating to pupils and parents at this level, but even then it's often because of outside help rather than internal structures.

### (e) To categorize

Young people tend to get themselves into categories or peer groups and the system is in danger of perpetuating an unhealthy view of others through the educational labelling routine. Often they fit, or they don't fit, according to their social background and upbringing.

## (f) To secularize

The missing dimension of our spirituality has made us two-dimensional people, forgetting that to have 'life' means we must include the spiritual in order to be whole. The attitude that 'everything can be explained' is a false attempt at an intellectual approach which is restrictive and limited. Exploring spiritual realities and life experiences is also a vital aspect of education.

# CONFRONTATION UNDER ATTACK!

There is always a danger, when summarizing, of being superficial. However, the kind of pressures parents, pupils and teachers alike have been under could fairly be summed up in the following way:

## Liberty...do it!

Anything goes, as long as you don't hurt anybody! We live in a free society so make your life choices. Problem is, as has already been stated, we are furnished with inadequate or slanted information which is not a healthy basis upon which to make those vital choices.

## Compatibility...try it!

In our urge to merge, we are ignoring important cultural and sociological differences which have given identity to communities for decades. Why are we afraid to recognize the differences in our society of colour, creed and sex and find strength and fulfilment in the different roles we have contributing to the whole.

## Availability...take it!

The temptation to get anything you want shouts from every street poster. But that's not the way it is. We must learn to live life by a different set of values.

# UNDER STARTER'S ORDERS!

### Spot the worker

So where is everybody? Where are the full-time schools workers committed to being effective in this area of ministry? Where is the vision of the church in this forgotten mission field right on our door step? If churches can support missionaries in other countries, what about raising finance to support missionaries in England? Some organizations have operated in a schools ministry for years, like British Youth For Christ, Scripture Union and Campus Crusade, yet we still have very few full-time people working in this area of tremendous opportunity.

I get tapes sent to me all the time from Christian musicians wanting opportunities to perform. I hear of other creative people in drama, mime and dance who are short of work. There are hundreds of young people wanting to serve God and yet not having the resources to do it. It's about time we took another look at our whole approach to youth work in this country and locked into the biggest opportunity we've ever had to reach thousands for Jesus.

### Plot the action

How do you get started? As a youth leader or a pastor, it is important to establish healthy contacts with the local schools. You will be surprised at the positive reaction you will get if you show a genuine interest in the school. Make supportive links with the Christian Unions that desperately need encouragement and resource ideas. Work out a strategy of action in your approach to the schools, firstly making vital contacts and building relationships and then, if you can communicate with young people well, asking for opportunities to be involved in assemblies, classroom presentations and lunchtime events. These ought to be prime target areas for every youth leader.

If you are unable to be involved during school time why not get people in who have expertise in this area of ministry to do a school mission linked to the local church?

If you do not see yourself as an up-front 'communicator', there is a real need for school counsellors to work alongside the teaching staff, and there are growing opportunities in this area also.

If you are a young person wanting to make an impact in your school, join, resurrect or start a Christian Union. I've seen highly effective CUs operating in many parts of the country, but I've also cringed at the image many have in their schools because of a lack of creative ideas or committed membership. Here are some guidelines that may be helpful for you in this situation:

1.  Create a good image for the CU. This can be done by choosing the right name, designing a good logo, having good publicity for events. Carefully construct a programme well in advance.

2.  Meet regularly, say once a week during the lunch break. Make it a time for building up the Christians and consolidating the work that is going on. Then, once a month, have a big splash event designed for your non-Christian friends. Make sure it's not wimpish! You can get ideas from places like Scripture Union, the Church Pastoral Aid Society and the Bible Society. British Youth For Christ and Scripture Union have contact with people working in a schools ministry who may be able to help also.

3.  Once a term have a school mission when, with permission from the head teachers concerned, you get involved with assemblies and lunchtime events, and also social and

religious studies lessons if you have a school worker available. What about getting a Christian rock band in to smash the myths young people have of Christianity? Have a good theme title for each mission and make sure that what you do is related to local churches, with a main event on neutral territory at the end of each week, when the gospel can be presented in a dynamic, creative and uncompromising way.

4. Make sure you have a leadership team that is committed and reliable and be sure to have a democratic way of choosing who should make up that team.

5. Establish links with local churches and get their leaders to come in from time to time to have an input into the consolidating, strengthening process of your group.

## Learn the approach

There are three basic ground rules in the schools operation.

1. Establish good relationships with the teaching staff and be careful not to antagonize or create ill feeling. For instance, if you are told you have eight minutes to do the assembly, make sure you take eight minutes and not a second longer! Be prepared to meet the staff during break-times in the staff room and show that you are human too! Be careful how you dress. It can be casual, but not scruffy. Respect the requests of staff and be ready to be adaptable.

That does not mean being walked all over and taken advantage of, but it does mean being as wise as serpents and harmless as doves!

2. Take an educational approach in your communication, not a preachy one. It is wrong to use the opportunity of having a captive audience to preach your favourite theological doctrine at them! Talk about issues that concern your audience, drawing out the facts of the argument and speaking from an alternative point of view. I've spoken elsewhere in the book about communication techniques and this would certainly apply here. I would want to deal with issues like the nuclear debate, law and order, sexual

relationships, the art of communication, human values, meaning and purpose in life and so on.

In a lesson period I would aim to say one main thing and approach this truth from a variety of angles using a variety of communication techniques: class involvement, simulation games, short dramatic exercises, blackboard visuals, music and lecture. I construct a lesson in the following way:

First, an introduction. This may be a conventional explanation of who I am, what I do and why I am there, followed by a general overview of the theme, or it may be a totally unpredictable, unconventional shock manoeuvre that will wake them up and drag their brains into first gear ready for the 'off'!

Second, I want to grab their attention and take them into the theme. I will do this by stating highly controversial things about the subject to stimulate their brains or by a creative bridge into the subject via a visual aid, simulation, song or drama.

Third, I will save the trump card until last, not drawing conclusions until I have built the communication 'bridge' into their thinking. Sometimes it works the other way, however. For instance, you could come right out with: 'In the next five minutes I'm going to prove to you that the Bible is true!' But if you say it, you'd better be able to do it!

Fourth, I will make sure I have a complete package and hit the target. This needs careful planning and timing, but works with practice. I usually have a whole range of ideas in my mind that fit into the main theme I am presenting, and at any time I can pick out an appropriate insert according to the intelligence level, response and receptivity of the class.

Fifth, I have found that it is best to avoid some controversial issues like evolution unless you are asked your opinion directly in a question time. It's often during this time that the pupils themselves will open opportunities for you to be much more direct than you would normally be allowed.

Sixth, I only work in a school situation if there is adequate back-up from the local church and an event, out of school time, to which we can invite the young people and be directive in our approach. So when I am drawing my conclusions in a lesson presentation, I will throw in the fact that if they want to hear more, they can come to an organized event, like a concert, and discover for themselves what we are talking about.

## Prepare for the aftermath!

The local church, in conjunction with the Christian Union, must be set up and ready to receive new converts and enquirers. Follow-up is a vital aspect of church growth. We have a responsibility to be spiritual parents to new spiritual babies and that takes time and patience.

Have home nurture groups ready to operate and get mature young people/youth leaders involved in running them. They should build a relaxed atmosphere where questions can be asked and things shared without fear of people feeling threatened or misunderstood. The 'Life' and 'Growth' studies from the Christian Publicity Organisation are good starting points for home groups. John Whitcombe has also produced a good book for nurture groups called *49 Steps*. This was produced in conjunction with BYFC.

It is also good wherever possible to link new converts with another Christian of roughly the same age and the same sex so that, on a one-to-one basis, they can meet and encourage one another. There are pointers and suggestions elsewhere in this book on counselling techniques for new Christians. There is also a wealth of material available to help you set up a training programme for nurture group leaders and counsellors. See recommended book list.

If we can recognize the potential of schools work and take hold of this opportunity, we would see a much more positive injection into our educational system as Christians begin to influence the workings of the machinery and point people to the ultimate meaning of their existence.

# 9

# *Rock Gospel: Cosmetic or Prophetic?*

Top of the agenda for many youth leaders over the last
couple of years has been the gritty issue of the use and
abuse of contemporary music. Young people are bombarded with 'hook lines' that captivate, insinuate and
motivate. Many are disturbed by the power wielded by the
latest pop idols and the lifestyles that generate feelings of
hostility to anything that appears to be 'establishment'. The
call to freedom has become for many a journey of despair,
disillusionment and death. The cynical commercialism of
the music business has corrupted many who were struggling
for stardom and captured millions who are struggling to
find their identity.

John Blanchard's book *Pop Goes the Gospel* caused a stir
on both sides of the pop music debate. Even though he
says, 'We have tried to work through the issues thoroughly,
carefully and honestly, without at any point being destruc-
tively critical of Christians who might not agree with us,'
the plain fact of the matter is that he blatantly and aggres-
sively attacks the music scene, naming names and casting a
slur on the Spirit-filled and God-ordained ministry of several
involved in gospel music. The tragedy of the book is that
while much of what is stated is good and should be taken on
board and thought through by all of us involved in music, it

comes from an author who is a million miles away from access to the whole truth and thus contains second-hand information, much of which is hearsay, inaccurate and inflammatory. Put in the hands of your average middle-aged church member, the book simply reinforces what they always hoped would be the case about the evils of pop music, thus adding a little more distance to the generation gap. Statements in the book like, 'Christian pop makes no spiritual, moral or ethical demands,' displays a gross ignorance of ministries that are operating in dynamic and prophetic dimensions, tackling the issues facing our society and pointing clearly to Jesus as the answer.

So what is it really all about? Should our young people turn all their contemporary rock albums into flowerpots? Should we censor what they listen to and watch? Should we encourage them to make alternative rock with a Christian slant? Having been involved in the business of making music as a full-time occupation for over six years, I think I'm ready to take the plunge and state my case!

## The facts

### The contemporary music scene

Radio 1 was established by the BBC in 1967, along with Radios 2, 3 and 4. It is now the most important outlet for contemporary music in Britain today. On TV *Top of the Pops* has become a pop institution watched by seventeen million viewers every week—all potential buyers of product. It's big business. Record companies can stand to make or lose millions of pounds on the strength of the success or failure of one artist. It's not surprising that many artists are processed and packaged in order to produce a marketable image to capture the mood of the buying public. Tom Bailey of the Thompson Twins has said, 'The only reason any band signs a deal is to get money...record companies have a pure and simple motive—to make money.' In the book *How To Get a Hit Record* by Ray Hammond, the tragedy of the pawns in the game is highlighted.

> During the peak periods of success, bands can be kept happy for months with a combination of ready cash, drugs, the natural ego food of becoming famous and, the last weapon in a manager's locker, sex.

He goes on:

> One of the major headaches for a manager is when one of the star performers falls seriously in love... for this reason managers set out to wreck any dangerous romances they see developing.

The average popularity life span of a top pop band is around two years, then starts the drift back into obscurity. Here is a telling quote from a book called *Inside Pop Music* compiled by the International Association of Fan Clubs.

> If your objective in making music is nothing more than a search for fame and fortune, be warned.... When the Beatles sang, 'Money can't buy me love,' they might have been singing the theme song for the whole of the rock 'n' roll business.

Many are sucked in by the possibility of glamour, fame and fortune and end up in compromising situations. Ray Hammond says:

> You'll have to steel yourself to do unpleasant things if you really want to make it. The road from obscurity to stardom is strewn with obstacles; each one will demand that you compromise a little of your integrity.

One well-known keyboard player is reputed to have said, 'My integrity is being held by my bank manager as collateral.'

Not surprisingly, there are many casualties in the world of pop music. The late Marc Bolan once said, 'I wish I could go insane or die sometimes, but I'm not allowed.' Sting, who has carved a career for himself via the internationally-known rock band 'The Police' has said scathingly, 'The best thing you can do in rock 'n' roll is die.' Janis Joplin, who died of a drug overdose, said, 'On stage I make love to 25,000 different people; then I go home alone.'

The case histories could fill several volumes. *Inside Pop Music* states

> There is virtually no mechanism within the industry for coping with the problems of an artist hopelessly ensnared by the traditional values of sex, drugs and rock 'n' roll.

The lucrative singles market is targeted towards fourteen- to nineteen-year-olds, who buy the bulk of records that go to make up the singles charts. Britain's first record sales charts began in the 1950s when they were compiled and published by the weekly music papers. There were a lot of hiccups with this system because of people trying to rig the sales figures, so at the end of the sixties the music industry decided to compile its own chart funded by itself, the BBC and the trade paper *Music Week*. An independent organization outside of the industry was employed to collate the sales data. So until 1983, the chart was compiled by the British Market Research Bureau which developed a system using a network of shops in key areas which supplied information. Now the Gallup Poll organization has taken over and their modern technology methods of processing data by special computer systems in selected shops is much more reliable. (Although every system can be worked!)

At the time of writing there are songs in the charts about the reality of love; over-indulgence; choosing between two partners; the wrong exploitation of people for personal gain; sexually explicit lyrics cancelling out the sentiments from the previous song; the heartbreak of a broken relationship; a call for faithfulness in a relationship or nothing at all; childhood pranks; the power of music; the fear of being conned; and a cry for truth.

I do not intend going into the all-too-familiar shopping list of bands graded according to 'X', 'PG' or 'U' rating! Other books have done that for us already, like Tony Jasper's excellent book *Jesus and the Christian in a Pop Culture*. Just as in every other area of life, our engagements with the dreaded 'world'(!) must be embarked upon through a Spirit-controlled life governed by the timeless laws of the kingdom. We too easily point fingers, turn our backs and quote things like, 'We must be in the world but not of it,' completely misinterpreting the real truth of that statement and using it as a camouflage to the real problem we have— we are completely out of our depth in the real world. Many of us have forgotten how to relate justice, truth and love to the nitty gritty affairs of modern life and completely forget the reason why we are here.

Tony Jasper says, 'My research suggests that the pop scene is not entirely bad. Beneath the sometimes tacky, even destructive elements of the music world, there is a longing for something spiritual.' Certainly there is more and more evidence to show these words to be true. More musicians and performers are declaring their faith in God openly and are having an amazing effect on their contemporaries. Our mindless concerns about the 'beat' and style of music threatening to mesmorize audiences and send them off into frenzies and orgies of violence is more a reflection on our personal taste in music than an accurate representation of the facts. Anyone who thinks style is the key factor should go to the Last Night of the Proms. The lifestyles of several well-known classical composers leave much to be desired.

Music is a powerful medium, but so is a football match. Anyone can pinpoint particular instances, performances, personalities or albums and highlight the anti-God emphasis and the dangerous effect of exposure to these tendencies. That is where spiritual discernment and wise action come into play. However, to eliminate all contemporary music with sweeping generalizations closes off the opportunity to make a real impact for the kingdom of God.

David Wilkerson in his leaflet *Confessions of a Rock 'n' Roll Hater!* says this:

> In all sincerity I preached against what I thought was compromise. I condemned a music style that was born in rebellion and idolatry. Looking back I wonder how many innocent young converts I hurt...I confess that I have been guilty of judging others by my own standards.

Then taking Romans 14:14 as a starting point, he goes on to underline that 'there is nothing wrong with rightfully using that which has been served to idols'. God in his creativity has given us so much to use to express who he is to the world.

## The Christian music scene

It's unfortunate that we have to have this sub-heading at all. For if the music that we are producing exists in the Christian youth sub-culture alone, we are in a ghetto situation and have not understood the meaning of the incarnation principle. Of course, some contemporary music is geared to 'ministering' to Christians, and there is a place for that. I am concerned, however, that we do not forget that 'infiltration' is a powerful form of communicating the love and justice of God to his world.

There are two kinds of Christian musician. Those who see their music as a tool to communicate God to people, and those who see themselves as musicians who happen to be Christians. I see both routes as valid expressions of creativity, but want to identify problems in both positions that need to be grappled with.

Those who see their music as a tool to communicate God to people tend to fall into three traps.

(a) A lack of professionalism in approach, presentation and outlook. There is no substitute for hard work, commitment and dedication. If we want to be effective, let's produce the goods well. God deserves nothing less.

(b) Superficiality in musical content. The old communication killer of 'religious jargon' creeps in to our music too. Let's observe our world through Spirit-filled eyes and then target our music accordingly.

(c) The trap of the 'Christian concert' circuit. I have watched many of my friends travel the dangerous route from what they perceive as 'grass roots ministry' in schools to the much sought after 'secular' music scene. Their reasoning is simple. If we can make it in the 'secular' scene, our potential audience will be so much bigger thus making the impact of our message much more effective. So many, however, have become high profile names in the small world of the Christian concert venue, and ended up missing the target completely and preaching to the converted. There is a mistaken idea that working in schools is where you begin in the Christian music business and that anywhere you go from this point is up. Rubbish! Where else can you regularly reach through live gigs a potential singles buying public of thousands every week? You can't get more 'secular' than that! The commercial repercussions are obvious although the spiritual impact is paramount. So where is everybody? I've already written a chapter on approaches to schools work, so get stuck in! You could still get a hit single! Tony Jasper again:

> Christian artists must not create a ghetto where they entertain the like-minded. They must not build cul-de-sacs of irrelevancy. Current pop culture calls out for people with new vision to challenge its negativism, its nihilism, its 'me' syndrome.

There are also dangerous traps awaiting those who see themselves primarily as musicians who happen to be Christians.

(a) The danger of compromising Christian standards for the sake of getting a contract. That spells spiritual suicide.

(b) The danger of alienation from the church, the family

of God, because of the fear of being misunderstood. This is an area we all need to work hard at because tragically many artists have been left out in the cold because of bigoted attitudes resulting from man-made values rather than the values of the kingdom of God.

(c) The danger of the argument that says, 'Just like a bricklayer who happens to be a Christian doesn't go around using his bricks to preach at people, so the musician who happens to be a Christian doesn't need to use his music to declare Christian truth.' I can buy this to a certain degree, but there is a fatal flaw to be overcome. A bricklayer is unlikely to have the kind of influence and public platform that a rock singer would have. This gives the rock singer an added responsibility whether he likes it or not. This does not mean that songs produced have to be Christian in content, but it does mean that he is an ambassador for Christ and therefore every interview, performance and public statement must reflect something of the nature of God. To camouflage faith because of a fear of being 'uncool' is a pathetic pandering to commercial pressures. There are so many bands preaching their messages loud and clear, it's about time we had the guts to come clean.

## The formulas

Here are a few words for those who may be thinking about starting a band or who are already involved in music but seem to be drifting.

### Getting behind the formulas

I have tapes sent to me all the time from bands and solo artists who are struggling to make ends meet, desperate to make inroads into the music scene but not getting the 'breaks'. There are a lot of really talented people around whose creative contribution to music could be quite significant. So what's the answer? How do you get started? How do you keep going?

There are hundreds of working bands that never make the Big Time, but who manage to scrape together a living from music. The few who do make it are often exploited, used and then drop out of the headlines after a couple of stabs at the top. Some bands manage to get to tour with a big name, but this is often achieved after an expensive arrangement that the business call a 'buy on'. It works like this. You agree to pay a large sum of money, which could be as much as £7,000 for the privilege of being seen on tour with the big boys! As the support band, you would often have to put up with second best in terms of sound and lighting co-operation, unless you were prepared to slip the right person a few quid as a bribe! All this sounds a bit like a soap opera theme, but that's the way it turns out for many. The glitter and glamour of life 'on the road' is not often the way you imagined it to be! Francis Rossi, guitarist with Status Quo, speaks for many when he says, 'At first it was a case of taking everything and anything just to keep playing.'

No formula is a guarantee of success, but there are general principles that seem to be common denominators in giving opportunities for the budding artist.

First, there are no short cuts. It is extremely rare for anybody to make it in the music business without having experienced the hard slog of gigging in small venues; humping precious equipment, which is not adequate but all you could afford, from place to place in a beat-up old van; playing to audiences that are often non-co-operative and unresponsive; being paid a pittance for your blood, sweat and tears, and grabbing a kebab on the way home as a consolation prize! I can recall many a time when we travelled halfway across the country to play in some dingy club and came away with a fiver and good intentions! If you feel you've got something to offer it's worth it. Dare I say, God will honour you if your motives are right. More of that later.

Secondly, the way you present yourselves during the whole set matters. It's not just the music that counts. I've seen brilliant musicians in action on stage who had no clue how to capture an audience and hold them. Conversely, I have watched in amazement as an artist without any great musical expertise grabbed an audience and created a dynamic atmosphere which ended in rapturous applause!

Stage presentation needs to be carefully thought through and rehearsed. Empty spaces between songs, with no visual or vocal impact to continue the momentum, can create a big-dipper effect and leave the audience bewildered. You are presenting a complete package in your concert set, so do it well.

Thirdly, try to write original material and make a demonstration tape of your music. It's possible to do this fairly cheaply these days by hiring an eight-track recorder and doing it yourself, or if you feel a little more ambitious, there are often special deals available at local recording studios that may be of help to you. If you do it this way, make sure you are adequately rehearsed before going into the studio—you won't want to waste precious time learning the material before recording.

Your demo tape will be useful in a variety of ways: sending to local concert promotors; sending out to folk interested in you playing at their venue. If it's good enough, it could be sent to local radio stations as a promo for your band. Then of course there are the record companies, if you are ready for that.

If you send your tape to a record company, make sure there are only three or at the most four songs on it; that you send short biographical notes and a good photograph. Don't forget to write your name and contact number clearly on the tape also. Some bands and management agencies employ 'pluggers' who will personally represent you to the record company's A & R (Artist and Repertoire) man. This is an expensive business so careful thought and wise counsel are needed before moving in this direction.

Many artists who have money and resources behind them go for demo videos of the band on stage rather than an audio cassette. If this is an option open to you, don't try to over-produce your video. Let it be an honest representation of your stage performance. It doesn't need to be an epic! Some clips of your performance put together by a good editor can do wonders. Remember, you are one of many trying to get the attention of the A & R man, so don't lose heart when you hear nothing! If it's what God wants, the right doors will open.

Fourthly, get a promotional pack together which will include press releases with latest news of the band, and do a regular mail-out of contacts with this information every three months, or when something major is about to happen. You will also need to make sure your Christian community is adequately informed so that people can pray for you and support you.

## Going beyond the formulas

We have looked at some of the general principles that should be thought through when launching out into the music business. We do need, however, to go beyond the cold mechanics of the situation and look at the deeper issue, without which everything will be in vain.

Make sure you have a solid spiritual base with people around you who are prepared to be a support group for you in prayer and guidance. Make sure you are firmly linked to a local church family so that you can receive the spiritual food that is vital if you are going to survive and be effective.

You need to discern with your spiritual leaders whether the Lord may be calling you into full-time work with the band. You need to discover exactly what your aims are and how these aims will be achieved. You need to think about a financial support base and a source of regular income. It may be right for you to do a year out on a voluntary team to get experience in a variety of settings. British Youth For Christ, Youth With A Mission, the Saltmine Trust, the London City Mission, Operation Mobilisation and Horizons are among those operating teams ministries.

## The frameworks

Whether you are using music as a tool to communicate something of the truth about God to people, or whether you are a musician who happens to be a Christian, there are certain criteria that need to be firmly established if what you are involved with is to be healthy and glorifying to the God we serve.

### Origination... where did it come from?

Whatever style of music you play, if it comes out of a life under the control of the Spirit of God, it will have a different kind of cutting edge. The lyrics may not be explicitly Christian, but there will still be an undercurrent emphasizing something of who God is or what he wants to say. The principle is highlighted by Jesus in the Bible: 'For the mouth speaks what the heart is full of' (Matthew 12:34).

I am often asked how I write songs. Again, there are no set formulas and everyone will develop their own methods. I have over fifty songs recorded on vinyl now, the same number again which have been used in public performance, and many, many more that never got past the waste paper basket! I like to write about current issues and things that have personally affected my life. This way what I am saying is firmly rooted in reality and avoids the danger of trying to communicate abstract and theoretical concepts.

My new song will start with a basic idea, phrase or 'hook line' that grabs my attention. This could be a newspaper headline or a phrase used by somebody in conversation. It could be words that I have strung together to illustrate a personal experience or observation. I attempt to create a visual image in my song writing that will cause the listener to 'see' a picture of what I am singing about. Some of my song titles help to explain what I mean: 'Hijack!'; 'Mayday!'; 'Signwriter'; 'Clockwork'; 'Robot Bomb'; 'A Matter of Honour'; 'Hit and Run!'; 'Shooting Wide of the Mark' and so on.

Let's look at two examples of using words to build a picture. The song 'Hijack!' uses this image to explain the fact that the Enemy has hijacked planet earth and the inhabitants can only expect release when the right person gives himself as a ransom...guess who!

Here are the first two verses setting the scene:

> Taken by surprise by the latest information,
> Hit between the eyes by something we should have seen
> before!
> Didn't realise the explanation,
> The subtle disguise of the bandit who pinned us to the floor!
>
> By careless mishandling we lost our direction,
> We threw away a fortune when we tried to fly alone,
> Looking all around for a solution,
> Mesmerised as we entered the forbidden zone!

If you want to know the end of the story, buy the record!

'Robot Bomb' talks about the mechanical way we treat each other, especially in the impersonal approach to war:

> Don't have to look at their face,
> You could watch a movie,
> Take a walk in space,
> Get a taste of glory,
> If the balance of power is in the right place,
> It's obvious we'll win the race!
> With the robot bomb! The robot bomb!
>
> Find a trivial pursuit,
> You could kill a few hours!
> It will take time to compute,
> While the mushroom flowers!
> We will accept no substitute,
> This is the only safe route,
> The robot bomb! The robot bomb!

The song goes on to talk about East-West conflict, the

horror of the charcoal beach, and finding your place in the Son!

So with a blank piece of paper before me, I would explore the theme with words and phrases scattered all over the page. I then begin to bring ideas together into verses and construct a framework for the song with a hook line that would occur like a punctuation mark throughout. This is the attention grabber and could be a repeated musical or vocal phrase. The problem with many songwriters is that they tend to be too wordy. I try to choose words carefully—I am not wanting to say everything in each song! An element of mystery stretches the mind and can develop thought patterns in the direction you have pointed. Try not to be too obvious and predictable. At the same time, if you want to write a hit single, avoid being obscure and go for the immediacy of the words and music.

If you are in touch with God by his Spirit, the material you produce will develop a cutting edge and grab attention. The origination of the material matters. If its source is in the heart of God, you have a powerful tool!

### Motivation... why are you doing it?

The debate about Christians in rock music often centres upon the difficulty people have with performers, claiming to be Christians, playing up to audiences and wallowing in self-glorification. I have watched well-known evangelists perform in a similar way. Even posing at the right moments in the message, so that the photographers can get the best angle!

Yes, we all have problems with our ego. So it comes down to the simple question, 'Why are you doing it?' The answer to the question could make or break you. Are you doing it for the money? The sense of personal power? Because you enjoy making music? Because you want to express yourself in creative ways? Because you feel you have something to say? Because you want to entertain people? Because you feel God has called you to this position and you desire to be faithful to what he has said?

However much we try to avoid the issue by using 'arty' language, the plain fact is that the last answer on the above list needs to come first. There may be other relevant factors, but that's the key issue if you claim to be God's person. We must aim for purity of motive, even if we miss the target most of the time. We must get God's help on this one. It does not mean that our stage performance from now on will demonstrate once and for all that Christians really are wimpish! It does mean that we must constantly remind ourselves of our awesome responsibility and answerability to God himself.

## Interpretation... what are you saying?

Remember that the impact of your performance as a complete package will be interpreted by the audience in certain ways. They will come away from that concert with an impression that will affect the way they think about vital issues. What you think you are saying may not be the message they receive. You may not intend to say anything—believing you are there solely to entertain. That's fine. But don't be naive enough to think that you are not in fact saying something by your attitude, approach and performance. Never forget that you are an ambassador—even if you are trying to be an undercover agent!

## Direction... where are you going?

When you lose your sense of direction, you begin to wander in the wilderness. There are many musicians in 'no man's land' who need to recover their sense of purpose. If you don't know where you are going, quit! Do something else before you fade away. Work out your target areas and give yourself time to reach them. Don't forget the vital element of prayer. God may be itching to say something to you that could revolutionize your life. Don't miss it!

### The fruit

We are looking for results. More importantly, God is looking for results. God brings the results as we walk with him. Here are three things about musical fruit we need to consider:

#### Negative or positive?

So much of contemporary music is negative: anti-establishment, anti-marriage, anti-authority, anti-parents, anti-religion, anti-war, anti-peace. In fact, it could be anti-anything so long as it encourages the natural tendency for adolescents to rebel against something.

We have a revolutionary message that can change the face of planet earth. Let's speak positively to our generation. That does not mean to say that we are 'pro' everything rather than 'anti' everything! It does mean that we are not prepared to walk around in circles. We are going to demonstrate our abundant life and express it in positive comments about our world that will result in change for the better.

#### Superficial or penetrating?

We want to get to the heart of the matter, not clip the surface and titillate the ear drums with nice clichés. We want to get beneath the gloss and get back to the spirit of punk...and I'm not talking about a musical style but a gut reaction. There is too much at stake to go skimming.

#### Cosmetic or prophetic?

For me, this is the key issue in the rock music debate. We need a three-megaton spiritual explosion in our world, to shake at the roots of corruption, immorality, injustice and violence. God has given us the power, the opportunity and the mandate. It's about time we stopped navel-gazing and in-fighting, and turned out together, working with God in the re-creation of society.

# 10

# *This Is the Green Submarine, Come in Big Red!*

There are many things that have left a vivid impression on me from my childhood years. I remember clearly experiencing every little boy's dream... to drive a big red London bus! I often travelled around London as a child and would always try to get the seat behind the driver's cab, so that I could watch, and advise of course, as he manoeuvred this great machine through the busy streets.

All these thoughts and impressions came rushing back as I trundled through the streets of Guildford driving our new acquisition to the youth work: a 1951 London double-decker bus. RT 3323 came with all the trimmings: genuine London Transport seats, destination rollers, the original colours, the distinctive bell. LYR 542 was on the road for Jesus!

Getting young people trained and mobilized is vital to the future of our church life in Britain. This chapter is all about the possibilities there are for young people to be involved in one-year voluntary projects, looking at the practical and spiritual implications.

### Mandate

Jesus never said we should sit in the security of our churches and have invitation posters stuck outside on the notice board to encourage people to join us. The commission given to the church was, and still is, to 'go into all the world and make disciples'. We have to recover the adventure of 'going' for Jesus into uncharted territory, and connecting with people where they are.

As a youth pastor I was concerned about this very issue. Although I was operating in a large, growing church, there were certain areas we were not reaching, so we needed to emphasize again the need to move out with the love and power of God. I remember an incident which took me by the scruff of the neck and made an impression on me that I will never forget. I was standing just outside the main auditorium of the church and looking in at the people singing a great song, '...here by the grace of God I stand.' As I looked at them I was aware of a presence behind me. I looked, and standing there was a young man who had had a lot of contact with our church. He arrived with a carrier bag containing all his possessions. He had just been made homeless for the fourth time.

There is something sobering about this occasion which ought not to pull the heart strings, but ought to drive us to our knees. There are fundamental questions that need to be asked. What can we do about the homeless, destitute and poor in our society? How can we reach those in our area who would never step inside a church?

Amos, the shepherd boy from Tekoa, a small town twelve miles from Jerusalem, became a prophet with a message that cut to the heart of the people of God and hit the nail on the head:

> I hate your religious festivals; I cannot stand them! When you bring me burnt offerings...I will not accept them...Stop your noisy songs; I do not want to listen to your harps. Instead, let justice flow like a stream, and righteousness like a river that never goes dry (Amos 5:21–24).

The prophet Micah, in similar mood, spoke the following often quoted words from the Lord:

He has showed you, O man, what is good; and what does the Lord require of you but to do justice, and to love kindness, and to walk humbly with your God? (Micah 6:8, Revised Standard Version).

The idea of using a mobile unit to reach people who might not have contact with the church is not a new one. However, the context in which we were using the bus, plus full-time team of eleven people, was unique. The church had the vision to get behind this project which had a variety of possibilities. It gave a new access into untouched and difficult areas where the very insular communities of people needed to know we cared; it gave a new visibility in terms of demonstrating the love of God to people, in a situation where they need not feel threatened or intimidated; it gave mobility so that we could move from one aspect of the ministry to another quickly and effectively, operating as a drop-in centre, or an exhibition centre, or a focal point for creative presentations; it gave opportunity for young people to be trained to reach others.

If we are going to fulfil the Great Commission there is a world on our doorstep that needs reaching. Through school missions, street evangelism, drop-in centres, involvement in community affairs and working with local churches in different areas, a mobile unit can have a powerful effect.

Before you start saying that this looks fine on paper, but you don't have the resources for this kind of thing, think again! A large chunk of the money we needed for the project during its first year of operations, came from outside the church. There are a lot of charitable trusts operating that will give to a community project of this kind. The key is to have a praying church, committed leadership, and bags of vision. The money can be raised.

A double-decker bus may not be what you need, but the principles involved are essential to apply:

(a) We need to reach out from the church into the community.

(b) We need some kind of focal point outside of the

church for operations.

(c) We need a way to give our young people (and older folk!) the opportunity of on-the-job training.

(d) We need to gather all of this into our fundamental target: to make disciples.

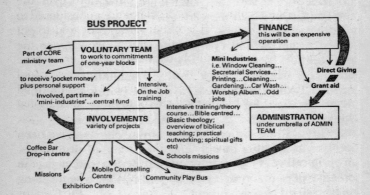

## Manifesto

The manifesto we had for our bus project and our youth work included:

### Claiming lost territory for God and holding it

There are vital areas that have been lost to the Enemy which we must recover for the glory of God.

The arts, once dominated by brilliant and innovative craftsman, musicians and painters within the church, is now dominated by those who have no real relationship with the source of creativity—the living God. If we are to be true in our desire to express the character of God to the world, that must involve creativity inspired by contact with the ultimate source of artistic expression—the Author of life himself. We need to be setting the agenda, not being dictated to by warped representations of truth and beauty.

Family life, ordained by God, centred around the relationship of a man and woman in marriage, is under threat. We desperately need to recover lost ground and fight the Enemy as he tries to destroy stable relationships and bring disunity, instability and despair.

Politics: we have lost valuable ground here over the years. When the church utters proclamations considered to be political statements, it is either ignored or told to get back in its place. In the past the church overstepped the mark when religion became a political affair rather than the correct emphasis of the people of God having a spiritual input into the running of the nation. We need to be informed and involved in the life of our local community and national life.

People, trapped by the tricks of the Enemy, have been enmeshed in countless fabrications, lies and distortions. It's time to expose the works of the Enemy and engage in spiritual warfare in the name of Jesus Christ. The meaning of life itself can only be found in relationship to the Creator of life, and fulfilment can only be obtained when we live God's way.

## Switching on lights in the darkness

Jesus said, 'Men loved darkness rather than light because their deeds were evil.' Jesus was the light of the world and everywhere he went he drew attention to anything that was 'dark'. He could not avoid it. Neither can we if we are children of the light. The prophets' approach was at the same time pessimistic and optimistic. They warned of judgement to come on all those who ignored the Lord God and rejected his ways. They also spoke of hope for the future when life is lived out with God at the centre.

Today we need to highlight the evils of our society what-ever danger that involves, for we can do no other if we are truly representing the kingdom of light. The prophetic words we utter can only be real as we live in close touch with our God and with one hand on the Bible and the other on the daily newspaper. We switch lights on not by pointing fingers at people, but by being like Jesus.

The Jeffrey Archer affair was in the news on and off for over a year. He resigned from politics because of an alleged relationship with a prostitute. The *News of the World*, in its usual gutter-press style, highlighted the story which was disputed strongly by the Archer family. As a result of the newspaper report, his resignation was inevitable. Another newspaper carried the headline: 'A Matter of Honour', which was ironically the title of one of Jeffrey Archer's books.

Whatever the rights and wrongs of this situation, and notwithstanding Mr Archer's victories over two newspapers, it worries me that people can be destroyed by accusation. The 'killer' press has power that it often uses irresponsibly. I wrote a song about this event. Some of the words go like this:

> Righteous fingers point out the facts,
> They have covered *their* tracks!
> Only one course of action is deemed to be right,
> When you live in the night.
>
> It's a matter of honour,
> When you look at the truth we're all to blame.
> A matter of honour,
> We started out right but we lost the game.
> A matter of honour.

So we need to live like Jesus did. Not being afraid to highlight the ills of society. But let's be careful that we don't make false accusations but learn how to attack the real Enemy.

### Letting Jesus live through us

Although God is never confined to one geographical location, he often allows his presence to have a special focal point of reference. The human brain cannot conceive the qualities and characteristics of a supernatural God and could never have any contact with him if it had not been for the fact that God took the initiative to reveal himself. We cannot dissect God as though he were some scientific formula or experiment. We only know what he has chosen to reveal.

So punctuated through the Bible we find references to God making contact with the world and revealing some aspect of his character. From time to time he has allowed himself to be identified in a particular geographical area. The progression runs through the Bible. First we read of God *in the garden,* making contact with his creation. Later we read of God *in the tabernacle*, the portable spiritual home of the people of God, that went with them on their travels through the wilderness. Isaiah's vision of God *in the temple* was another progression of God taking the initiative to reveal himself to his people. Moving over into the New Testament we see that God was *in Christ*, reconciling the world to himself.

The incredible truth we must learn to grasp and apply is this: we are now the temples of the living God. He chooses to live in us and work through us. It's a staggering and sobering thought! 1 Corinthians 3:16 says: 'Surely you know that you are God's temple and that God's Spirit lives in you!'

Ezekiel chapter 43 talks about the characteristics of the temple. Although it is referring here to the physical temple, if we are now the spiritual temple of the living God, the same characteristics must apply. Ezekiel mentions at least five aspects that we need to allow to filter through into our lives and experience as we take on board the manifesto of the kingdom of God.

The temple was the place of God's glory. The word 'glory' carried with it the feeling of density or heaviness. It's a very powerful, effective, forceful illustration of God. In Exodus we read of the Israelites seeing the glory of God as 'a consuming fire'. The prophet Isaiah speaks of the appearance of the glory of God: 'And the glory of the Lord shall be revealed, and all flesh will see it together.' Handel's musical interpretation of those words gives a feeling of excitement, joy, wonder and awe in anticipation of this amazing experience to come.

John says in his account of the life of Jesus, 'And we saw his glory, glory as of the only Son from the Father.' As God exhibits his glory in our lives, we will have a new cutting edge and that will result in his glory being released in the world.

The temple was the place where the throne of God was set up. No other gods have the right to usurp that throne, but still many of us live as though God were not Lord of our lives at all. If he is going to live through us, he must be in control.

The temple is the place where the holiness of God is displayed. Holiness is a word meaning separation, not alienation. It is all about absolutes. There can be no compromise in God and God expects no less from his people. That is why the command is clear in the Bible. God says, 'Be holy for I am holy.' Peter quotes this Old Testament verse when speaking about the need for holy living (1 Peter 1:13–16). Holiness means being different. Living God's way in his truth with his justice. Holiness means being decisive. No compromise. No double-talk. No back tracking. Holiness means being dangerous. This kind of life must affect and challenge us.

The temple is the place where sacrifices are given. Jesus has paid the last sacrifice for sin on the cross. There are still sacrifices to be given, not dead ones but living. You and I, to be precise! Paul told the Roman church that giving ourselves as living sacrifices is our 'spiritual worship'.

Finally, in Ezekiel 43, the characteristic forming the climax of the chapter is that of worship. We need to rediscover the art of true worship that transcends human formulas into the realm of supernatural encounters with God.

Letting Jesus live through us is part of God's special plan for all his people. We are the body of Christ and all have a different part to play. God holds everything together by the activity of the Holy Spirit making it all real and alive.

## Building bridges in a divided world

The final part of the manifesto was all about bridge-building. Having a desire to 'close the gap' and make personal relationships with people that go beyond the superficial. There is no doubt about the fact that we live in a divided world. Divisions bring misunderstanding, hatred and war. Look at Northern Ireland, the Middle East, Sri Lanka, the Berlin Wall, the Great Wall of China, the East/West divide, rich and poor, privileged and underprivileged. There are cultural divisions, spiritual divisions, sociological divisions. As Christians we are called to be 'priests', being like bridges between people and God. An awesome task but a God-given responsibility.

## Mobilization

We identified several young people who had the potential for operating in a team. After spending time with them and praying through the issues and demands that would inevitably come, we settled on ten people to form a teachable group for the launch of our first year on the bus project. We also invited a young lady to join us to be my assistant and take care of the administration which was considerable.

The excitement grew as plans were made for the launch on September 14th 1986. Some of the team members had jobs to leave and a new lifestyle to prepare for. They would be earning £35 per week, £20 of which would go to their host families for food and accommodation. They had to raise this money themselves. It doesn't take a great mathematician to work out that over the course of the year, each member would need to raise £1,820, or to put it more dramatically, £20,020 for the whole team! It is staggering how God provided the money through sponsors, charitable trusts and gifts from engagements undertaken.

I put together a course of study called BUSTOPS covering five main areas:

*(a) Communication:* understanding the culture in which we live, exposing the persuaders, exploding the myths, hitting the target areas, delivering the goods and many other areas that we have in fact tackled in this book.

*(b) Christian doctrine:* a bird's-eye view of basic Christian truths to give a fundamental understanding of the character of God, the Person and work of Jesus Christ and the Person and work of the Holy Spirit.

*(c) Counselling:* how to answer objections, how to lead someone to Jesus, how to deal with specific problems.

*(d) Apologetics:* evidence for the Christian faith.

*(e) Personal development:* taking an internal view and through group work, interraction and teaching, to discover gifts God had given and how to use them.

Unlike most other teams I have worked with over the years, this one was highly creative and full of individuals! There was Jo, full of vitality who, in addition to her involvement with drama, displayed a real heart for people. Pete took the lead in drama and developed a powerful up-front communication gift as the year progressed. Tracey took the lead in the area of dance and with Nicky and Christina put together some inventive and effective dance routines that spoke volumes in the numerous presentations they did. Mark had a real gift in communicating visually, so took on the responsibility of promotion, artwork and public relations. Stuart and Helen, both superb musicians, formed the musical input and developed over the year into a high-quality performing band called 'Sivan'. Dave was the technical whizz kid and also played keyboards for worship. Jackie was an ex-science teacher who became the leader of the team. Her qualities as leader grew as the different circumstances she faced stretched her faith and ability! She also made a great bus driver! Monica, my assistant and administrator of the project, showed her organizational ability and helped to hold things together in what was a chaotic, exciting, demanding, frightening, rewarding year!

For a pilot project, something never attempted before on this scale with a local church, things went well. There were teething troubles and tensions from time to time in the team which are inevitable in an operation of this nature. There were things we would change a second time round, but we saw the principles outlined earlier in the chapter being worked out. The 1986 team have moved on now. One to Bible college, three have got married, four back into secular employment, one into the professional music scene, two into other forms of full-time Christian work. They have all gained valuable experience, not only in areas of communication and creative arts, but also in relating to one another in caring relationships. Their input lives on as the bus continues to trundle around the streets of Guildford and the surrounding areas.

There are a growing number of opportunities for young people to get 'on-the-job training' in evangelism. British Youth For Christ run a teams ministry, with young people giving a year to work alongside a local church in a team situation. Oasis, the trust set up to support Steve Chalke's ministry, is also developing a teams ministry concentrating on the major cities of our nation. Youth With A Mission are well known all over the world for operating with teams of young people, putting them into a variety of situations for faith-sharing and training experience. Many of the missionary organizations also have opportunities for short-term as well as long-term service and many have gained valuable insight into the needs of the Third World through projects with organizations like Tear Fund.

We should encourage our young people to get involved. It's not an easy option. Hard work, dedication and financial hardship are things to be expected. Many have the opportunity to take a year out after leaving school and before starting work, or after leaving university. Others may be feeling the specific call of God into full-time work, and a year like this can explore and test the calling of God on their lives. Spiritual back-up and support is vital for the individuals involved. Young people with this kind of experience can often be fed back into their local church situation in a leadership role, to help them relate what they have learned in their own home situation.

## Management

If you are thinking of starting a voluntary project in your area, here are a few tips that may help you on your way:

(a) It's important to evaluate your situation and the resources you already have as well as doing some research into the needs of the area in which God has placed you. Have someone do a written report outlining the specific needs of the area having done a survey and contacted the local authority, social services, police, probationary service and voluntary organizations already in operation. Keep all these people informed of what you are doing.

(b) Impart the vision God is giving you to the local church. Do not move on it until the people of God you are joined with share the same vision.

(c) Do your financial homework. What exactly do you want to set up? What will the origination costs be? The preparation costs? Although our double decker maintained its authenticity and originality, we took all the seats out upstairs and put carpet down using sag bags for seats. We had a TV and video at one end. Downstairs we kept the seats, although we did rearrange them, turning the area into a coffee bar/lounge with a coffee machine. All the electrics were worked via a powerful Honda generator, and we installed a heating system run on propane gas.

Then, of course, there are the ongoing running costs. What is involved to fulfil legal requirements? Where will the money come from? It's worth visiting your local library and going through the book *The Directory of Grant-Making Trusts* to find possible avenues of raising money. Also check out the Job Centre for other possible ways of raising finance for a voluntary project. If you are using people who have been unemployed for a certain length of time, the Government have various schemes that would help.

(d) What personnel are needed? Where will they be drawn from? Who will train them? Who will be the team leader? Where will they live? Who will feed them? What about transport? How will they relate to the church? Do they have a long-term goal beyond the 'year' project? Can you help them achieve that goal? How many should there be on a team? What responsibilities will each one have?

(e) Work well in advance, preparing a phased programme building up to the project. Make sure it fits into an overall strategy being worked out in your church.

(f) Make sure you have a tight administrative unit which will keep tabs on what is going on: writing the letters, communicating with the church, holding the financial accounts, putting together the prayer bulletins, handling the engagements. There are other practical considerations also. If you are thinking of starting a mobile unit of some kind, then the Fire Officer needs to be consulted and the local authority if food stuffs are to be prepared on location. At the time of writing, a double-decker bus does not come under the regulations governing Public Service Vehicles if it is a voluntary project and fare-paying passengers are not being carried. Similarly, if operated for non-commercial reasons, an HGV licence is not required. This means that with adequate training, a person can drive a double decker on a normal driving licence with a restricted number of passengers.

(g) Make sure you have adequate back up following operations in the area: a follow-up strategy, nurture groups, suitable literature, the right people involved.

(h) Promotion and publicity are also vital aspects to be

thought through and set up. Keep regular contact with local press outlets, issuing regular press releases. Local radio stations are always on the look out for stories of local interest. Your project must have a good theme title and logo, well designed and presented. Posters, stickers, hand-bills, balloons and so on can be used for an eye-catching launch.

(i) Don't be afraid to continually assess and evaluate the progress of the project and the problems encountered. Learn from mistakes. Sharpen up the jagged edges, keep the target areas clearly in focus. Maintain a long-term strategy that can see beyond the immediate into future possibilities and developments.

(j) Enlist the help of older folk in the church who may have expertise in different areas: mechanics, artists, designers, electricians, painters, drivers. They would love to be involved.

## Conclusion

By the way. You've probably been wondering what 'The Green Submarine' is all about. No, it's not another hair-brained scheme to convert deep-sea divers. It's the name the young people lovingly gave to my partly-customized Bedford CF van. With a round blown window in the side it looked like it could operate as a submersible! And the CB radio was really useful!

# 11

# *And Now, What You've All Been Waiting For!*

The heart cry of most youth leaders is, 'Help! I need some new ideas!' This chapter will be crammed full of tips and ideas for creative programming. There are a few things that need to be said, however, before we start digging into material that could be used.

## Explore

First, take a look at the resources you have and make a list of them. Look in the loft, the spare cupboard, on top of the wardrobe, anywhere you think there might be potential props lurking.

Secondly, have a think about what you need. It's worth bearing in mind that you can often get help from the local authority if what you are doing is deemed to be for the good of the community.

Thirdly, explore the approach that you take with the young people. There are certain guidelines to work with:

(a) You are not there to spoon-feed them. We all have a need to achieve. In our TV age that need is often short-circuited. That's why there is often so much apathy and lack of motivation. Snazzy programmes are not always the perfect solution to getting your group mobilized.

(b) Be aware of those not wanting to be involved in the planned activity. It's a time consuming affair 'noticing' people, but it's a 'must' in youth work. There is a reason why people are dropping out; there is no substitute for personal attention.

(c) Keep firmly at the front of your mind the aims and objectives of your event. When there is no goal, the group will wander and die.

(d) Be careful in planning and preparation. When things don't work properly, young people are turned off. Remember that 'spontaneity' launched out of a prepared framework is very effective.

(e) Don't ignore failures and mistakes. Don't stop being adventurous—you may become boring—but be sure to evaluate what you do and learn from it.

(f) Be prepared to work within your limitations (space, finance, equipment, expertise) but don't be afraid to think big for God! Plan big projects using the young people themselves in delegated roles.

(g) Do not flog a dead horse! New ideas will naturally take time to take root. In any radical reshaping process there will be those who will drop out. You can't please all the people all the time! But if something is blatantly not working and you're not achieving objectives, close it down and do something else (like pray!). God knows the next step.

(h) In your programming, be aware of other events in your locality. There is no point in duplication. We are not in this to compete with other church groups on the most 'with it' programme!

### Examples

In this section I want to give some ideas of material that has proved effective in different situations. They may trigger off a whole batch of other creative ideas as you capture something of the excitement of communicating the truth.

Some ideas I have used in a variety of settings, but for the purpose of a digestible structure, I will slot them under the best heading.

## (a) Small group situations

These include school classrooms, youth groups and Christian Unions. Simulation games are a very effective way of communicating truth and go down well in a small group. These are activities designed to get people involved in the learning process, a very effective way of teaching.

### Air raid shelter

This will help the group to see by what criteria they value other people, and discover their own self-worth.

*Phase one.* Have the people divide into groups of about eight and then appoint a leader for each group.

*Phase two.* Each person in the group must take on an identity (secretary, factory worker, unemployed person, nurse, politician, rock singer, or anything else they choose). Then, directed by the leader, each individual must explain to the rest of their group what role they have chosen and how they fulfil that role.

*Phase three.* You then explain to the whole gathering that there has been a nuclear war, and they are sitting in an air raid shelter. Out of the eight people in their group, only four people can remain in the safety of the shelter because of a lack of provisions for them all. Under the direction of the group leaders, each group must decide who should stay. Encourage individuals to plead their case and watch the results.

*Phase four.* Have a report-back session, getting each team leader to say who they chose and why.

*Phase five.* Get the groups to discuss a couple of relevant questions about how we attribute worth. They could be questions about abortion or euthanasia. Again have a report-back session.

*Phase six.* In some situations it would be appropriate at this point to encourage the groups to share and pray for one another.

This simulation in a school classroom can be an effective way of opening up a discussion on the real value of people in the sight of God. There are many variations on this idea which can be adapted to your own situation.

## Paper towers

Split the group into smaller units of about five or six people. Give each group a newspaper, a roll of Sellotape, a ball of string and a pair of scissors. Tell them they have five minutes to discuss among themselves how they will construct a tower using the materials provided. They must not, however, commence the building until you give the signal. After five minutes, tell them this is a lesson in communication and they must now build their towers without a word being spoken. Communication exercises are interesting and helpful in building relationships within the group, and also in helping people learn how to relate to others. Again there are a whole host of such games.

## Follow the leader

Again in groups of about eight, ask people to organize themselves into lines with the most important at the front and the least important at the back. Each one will have a piece of paper on which they write their number in the line, the most important being number one and so on. When they have done this get them to discuss together how they felt about this operation. Did they feel threatened? Cheated? Fearful of conflict?

Now tell the group you want them to elect someone they think would make a fair leader. They each have the number of votes according to the number on their piece of paper. So number one only has one vote whereas number eight, of course, has eight votes and so on. Someone with several votes must use all of these on one person. When the votes are cast, get them to discuss the outcome and this exercise by saying how they feel about the turn of events in the game, what they feel about votes given to those viewed as being least powerful and what they feel makes a fair leader.

This simulation is suitable to lead into a variety of themes: our reactions to authority, power structures, qualities of leadership, value of people, need for equality, etc.

## Paper aeroplanes

Get the group to make paper aeroplanes. Test-fly them and then ask each person to estimate how far they could fly the plane if they were allowed time to modify and improve it. They must publicly state their goal. After giving time for the modifications to take place, get folk to demonstrate their planes in flight. Do they reach their goals? Did they ask others to help and advise them in their modifications? Did they over-estimate what they could achieve? Did they under-estimate? Did the fact that they had publicly to state their goal make them more determined to reach it?

One of the major problems in youth groups is a lack of motivation and direction. This can be a great discussion starter on this vital theme.

## House of cards

A similar exercise to the one above, but this time people must estimate how high they can build using a pack of used cards.

There are hundreds of simulation game ideas that can be used in groups to great effect. Bob Moffet has brought together from various sources useful material in his books, *Power Packs* (Scripture Union) and *Crowd-Breakers* (Pickering & Inglis). Another book of around eighty simulation ideas is called *Games for Social and Life Skills* by Tim Bond (Hutchinson). Christian Aid have a useful activity called 'The Trading Game' which can be used to highlight the problems of the Third World.

Drama is a brilliant way of helping people remember truth. Try splitting the group up into teams and giving them each a proverb. Allow ten minutes for each team to produce a drama depicting the proverb.

The following is a typical classroom presentation. Taking the theme of 'rules' ask who has the right to make the rules.

Ask all the people with watches on to check the time and to shout it out. Everyone will have a slightly different interpretation of the time. How can we know what the time really is? Get them to give you some ideas. Draw a circle on the blackboard with 'Greenwich' written inside. Draw lines coming out of the circle and on the end of each line write a different suggestion of how we can discover the time. Point out that however good the suggestions, the only way to get it right is to have an absolute: Greenwich. If everybody puts their watch right by the 'absolute' at the same time, then they will agree with each other.

Now replace the word 'Greenwich' with 'God'. Explain the concept. We all have different ideas about what is right and wrong. Wars are fought over issues to do with different ideas about 'rights'. If we look at each other for the answer, we cannot agree, there is simply chaos. We need an 'absolute' and God is the only one who has the right to make the rules. He made us. He knows how we tick (forgive the pun with Greenwich!). When he is at the centre, we look upon each other in a different light.

Attack the theme from different angles using different creative methods. Don't over-expose the gospel. God can take care of himself! Be direct without being preachy.

Use a simulation game to illustrate rule making. For instance, ask people to imagine in groups they are on a desert island. They must make the laws for the island that will be most beneficial to the long-term security of the inhabitants. Give them time to decide. What are the rules they choose and why? Have an open discussion and explore the different approaches the different groups had.

## (b) Large-group presentations

These include school assemblies and youth services.

### The gun illustration

This was explained in chapter two, and is an illustration which works really well in school assemblies. It's one they won't forget.

### The chess game

Taking a phone on stage with you, have a mock conversation with an imaginary friend who is trying to explain the game of chess to you. You get muddled when he speaks of castles (what size?), the Queen (which one?), the bishops (they get in everywhere!). With a little imagination, you can have a lot of fun with this one-man sketch. The idea, of course, is that the ideal situation is for your friend to come round to your home and show you how to play the game of chess. Explaining it from a distance is impossible.

Then apply the sketch: God did not shout at us from a distance, but actually became involved in human life in the Person of Jesus Christ. He came to where we are in order that he might take us where he wants us to be. That's the uniqueness of Christianity above any other religious belief: God comes to where we are in Christ.

### Trust exercises

There are a lot of these, but here is one that goes down well in an assembly/large group situation. Ask for six volunteers from the audience. They must be male 'heavies'. Get them to form two groups of three in facing pairs. Then they must reach across and take the hand of their respective partner. You then say that you trust them to catch you, and you are going to take a run, and jump into their arms. This works well—if they catch you! It even works well when they don't! I once tried this exercise with some sixth formers and they thought I was bluffing, so when I launched myself at them, they all moved out of the way! I must confess I was angry and turned on them in front of the hushed audience, 'That was unforgivable,' I said. 'I trusted you and you let me down!' Next time they caught me and it was a great lead into talking about relationships that let you down—something all young people know about—and of course the one relationship that never fails.

## The fireman

This works well with a younger age group (first and second years). Get a young lady to come and stand on a chair. She must imagine she is on a burning building, and shout for help. You then need a 'fireman'. Get a volunteer to run round the hall making 'siren' noises! He then winds the ladder up, but unfortunately it is too short. So from the top of the ladder he calls to the girl, 'Jump, and I will catch you!'

She replies, 'I've always admired the fire brigade. How strong you are, how reliable! Obviously you can catch me and I have every confidence in you.'

'Then please jump,' says the fireman!

'But I most sincerely, honestly do believe that you can catch me,' says the girl. 'Have you noticed the view from up here, beautiful scenery. Birds are singing...what a lovely day for climbing ladders.'

By this time the fireman is getting frustrated. The problem is she believes the fireman can catch her, but will not jump.

Many people believe in God but are not saved because they have not trusted him. At this point you can extend the illustration by getting another person to come up the ladder and give a 'testimony' of how they were saved by jumping into the fireman's arms, and then finally get the audience to do a countdown, and encourage the volunteer's to act out the jumping! There can be interesting results!

### (c) Open air communication

#### Egg roulette

This is an old favourite of many. Have a box of six eggs, five of which have been hard boiled beforehand, leaving only one raw. Get a volunteer from the crowd to come and choose an egg. Then another volunteer comes and smashes the egg over the person's head! If it is the raw egg, it can be fun! The illustration is obvious. How long will we play games with life and death? There are vital decisions that every person must make which will affect their eternal destiny.

#### Henrietta the glove

Another old favourite, with several variations. Tell the crowd you have your pet with you, and after some speculation produce your pet glove. Explain that this pet can do tricks and if the crowd will count one, two, three, it will jump one metre. Of course nothing happens. This can be done several times to build expectation! Now you must relate to your glove. Explain to the audience that the reason why the glove will not jump is probably because it doesn't feel loved. So tell it how much you love it! Still no reaction. Perhaps it is because it needs discipline. Scold it! Still no reaction. Then put the glove on your hand expressing your surprise that it now moves at your command.

Obviously the application is that a glove is made for a hand and does not fulfil its purpose outside of that. We are made for God, but are empty and lifeless until God steps into our lives and takes control. Then we start to live the way the Creator designed for us.

#### Open air campaigners methods

Using a sketchboard is highly effective and well worth taking time to perfect. With a little bit of imagination and thought, everyday objects can be used effectively to create a visual impact and lasting impression on an audience.

There are many books around these days with ideas on how
to use objects in communication.

### (d) Children's services

*Weight watchers!*

Have a pair of scales at the front and invite children to come
and stand on them. Everyone ends up being eight stone! (A
little pushing and shoving achieves this result!) Ask if any
of the adults would like to weigh eight stone!

Ask one of the cute kids to come and stand on the scales.
After making sure he too weighs eight stone, give him two
things to hold, one in each hand. Then offer him a chocolate
bar! Tantalize him with the thought that he could have it,
but unfortunately he has no way of holding it, so he had
better go back to his seat.

Talk about Hebrews 12:1–2 '. . . let us also lay aside every
weight and sin which clings so closely, and let us run with
perseverance the race that is set before us' (Revised
Standard Version). Get two volunteers to come out to
demonstrate ways in which sin affects us. Get one to give
the other a piggy back. The first thing that sin does is hold
us down like a heavy weight. The longer we carry it the
heavier it gets! Then get them to reverse the procedure.
Sometimes we try to get on top of sin, or to pretend it isn't
really there. But it will not go away! Then get the two of
them to have an arm wrestling match. Sin can be like this
too, a continual fight going on inside. Talk about ways in
which this works out in life. Then get the original cute kid
back on the scales holding the weights. What must he do to
get the chocolate bar? Put down the weights! Let him do
this and give him the bar!

Jesus died to take the weight of our sin on his own
shoulders. We can be free to receive his forgiveness and the
gift of new life when we lay our sin at his feet.

## Storing your ideas

Over the years I have developed hundreds of illustrations for a variety of applications. I need a filing system to help me find the right approach for the right situation.

How about starting a filing system to store your illustrations and ideas? So often you might hear an idea or be inspired by a newspaper article and then forget it or lose it. I use a simple system that works well. I have a card index with topics written on cards in alphabetical order. Under 'D' for instance I have cards for 'discipline', 'doubt', 'disease', 'drama', 'drugs', 'dance', etc. On each card I have a series of numbers referring to the topic on the card. These numbers take me to a larger filing cabinet holding A4 size folders. In the folders are newspaper articles, ideas written on scraps of paper, magazine clips, simulation game ideas, illustrations and so on. Each item has a number on it. This number is recorded on the card related to the topic in question. Some clippings may come under several headings. That's OK, just put the number on the cards appropriate. This way, when you want an illustration for a certain subject, look at your card for that topic and then go to your A4 filing system for your numbered resource.

## Expertise

There is a growing body of expertise in this country with resources being developed to match the specialized needs of youth work. The following is not an exhaustive list by any means, but it represents some of the avenues I have used for constructive and useful resource material.

*'This Generation Youth Evanglism File'*—produced by British Youth For Christ—is packed full of information which is a must for every youth leader. (Cleobury Place, Cleobury Mortimer, Nr Kidderminster, Worcs DY14 8JG.)

*Pathfinder Training and Resource Manual*. Useful ideas updated at regular intervals from the Church Pastoral Aid

Society, 32 Fleet Street, London EC4Y 1DB.

*Gospel Light Youth Resources* are good quality materials and excellent for taking relevant bits from the masses of material available and constructing it to fit your requirements (27 Camden Rd, London NW1 9LN.)

*Christian Publicity Organisation.* Brilliant for PR material, tracts, posters, message leaflets.

*Scripture Union.* A good selection of audio/visual materials including the following resource books: *Youth Group How To Book, Try This One* (3 books), *Serendipity* youth series. *Jam* is an excellent monthly magazine for young teenagers including daily Bible reading ideas.

*Bible Society.* A good selection of practical 'how to' books.

*Contact for Christ.* A Bromley based organization which assists local churches and organizations in running events with the vital aspect of follow-up. Also have some good follow up materials available (7 London Rd, Bromley, Kent).

*Bob Moffett* has gathered together a lot of ideas in his compilations, *Power Packs* (Scripture Union) and *Crowd-Makers* (Pickering & Inglis).

*Care Campaigns.* Excellent for giving your young people an informed view of what's happening in our society (21a Down Street, London W1Y 7DN).

*Tear Fund* provides an informed view of what is happening around the world, and useful resource material for action. (100 Church Road, Teddington, Middlesex TW11 8QE.)

*Youth With A Mission.* Great opportunities for short and long term service for young people. (Holmstead Manor, Staplefield Road, Cuckfield, W Sussex RH17 5JF).

For the many other organizations which specialize in material for communication, see the *UK Christian Handbook* produced by MARC.

## Expectations

This chapter has contained a few key ideas to get your mind into gear! There are many possibilities, but we need to work hard to develop material that will be relevant and memorable to the people with whom we are communicating. Have a big expectation of what God can do through you, and keep your ear to the ground and your filing system at the ready for any new creative ideas that you pick up along the way.

# Postscript

It's incredible what people believe.

Sometimes people encouraging the belief know themselves that it is false.

For instance, there have been some notable April Fool's pranks played on the general public over the years! In 1957, Richard Dimbleby convinced thousands in a TV news report, that spaghetti grew on trees! In 1976, Patrick Moore convinced many that, because of a certain alignment of planets, if people carried out a certain procedure, they would find themselves being lifted off the ground. Many wrote in claiming they did have the experience and Patrick Moore confessed later that it was all a practical joke!

Sometimes, however, those encouraging the belief actually believe it themselves.

George Adamski claimed that he had met a man from Venus dressed in a tracksuit who warned him of the dangers of using atomic weapons. He also claimed that he had been to the planet Saturn. It took him nine hours travelling at an incredible twenty million miles an hour. He said that Saturn was a fairyland world of music and picturesque cities. Adamski's revelations went public in the 1950s and many have read his books believing them to be authentic records of actual events.

Von Däniken was a household name a few years ago and became a millionaire from the sales of his books. He claimed that God must have been an astronaut and that he had proof of this. Subsequently, every reliable scientist researching his findings has stated the absurdity of the conclusions he has come to. Many people, however, have been taken in by his books.

Take the pyramid of Cheops for instance. If you measure the height of it and multiply your answer by a factor of one thousand million you get the answer 98,000,000 miles! This of course is quite close to the distance that the earth is away from the sun (on average 93,000,000 miles). This cannot be a coincidence, Von Däniken argues! Obviously the pyramids were designed by beings from outer space!

It's amazing what people believe.

This book has been all about 'closing the gap'. Although the Christian faith makes sense and tackles the real issues facing the human race, many are searching in other places for the truth about life. It seems, with a little bit of ingenuity and imagination, you can get people to believe almost anything! Face them, however, with the challenge of Christianity, backed up by millions of lives that have been transformed by a living Jesus and the overwhelming evidence for the authenticity of the Bible, and there is a blockage in the works. It is vital that we learn how to close the gap, for people are eager to know but they are hearing the wrong message.

## 1. The credibility gap

In the eyes of the world around, the church says one thing and does another. It has lost credibility. We must regain the ground by being like Jesus, living like Jesus, reacting like Jesus, serving like Jesus, loving like Jesus.

## 2. The communication gap

Our secret code language must go! There is nothing 'holy' in camouflaging truth! We need to work hard to understand why people misunderstand and misinterpret what we are saying. What do we actually mean when we speak our religious formulas? How can we express our God creatively to the world he made?

## 3. The cultural gap

Like Paul in Athens, we need to make an effort to understand the culture in which we live and indeed the multinational nature of our society. The message of Jesus cuts right across barriers of race, colour, creed and culture, so let's be careful that we are not simply promoting a Westernized Christianity devoid of spiritual reality.

## 4. The confidence gap

We have a great God! We must be willing to be pioneers and prove his power if ever we are going to convince others that he is alive. As we launch out and burn the bridges behind us, exploring new depths of power and love, so our confidence will grow in our living God who longs to operate more and more through the lives of human beings sold out for him!

There has never been a more exciting time in history in terms of the opportunities to move out for God in power. Let's make sure we don't miss them!

# Christian Youth Work

## by Mark Ashton

*Large format paperback*

They say it all began in the forties: the teenage phenomenon. Brought up on a diet of rock and roll and the latest fashion, courted by the consumer society, and now jilted by mass unemployment – today's teenager faces the most fast-changing, high-tech society the world has known.

This book takes account of modern thinking and attempts to match what we know about young people today with what the Bible reveals about 'adolescence'. No church will be able to plan and activate its ministry to youth without coming to grips with the issues examined here.

Mark Ashton's thorough and careful analysis provides church leaders, youth workers and parents with an agenda for discussion and a manifesto for action. Aware of important social trends and young people's needs, he combines this knowledge with a strong and vibrant commitment to biblical truth and pastoral care.

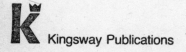

Kingsway Publications

# Keep in Step

## by John and Sue Ritter

Society moves on. Kids (that's the bigger ones, also known as 'teenagers') often lead the way—always moving, asking questions, looking for something.

If the world is moving, then Christians can't stand still. We have to be there when the questions are asked, when the hurts are felt and the fears revealed.

Not at arm's length, but in there with them.

Not looking the same, but offering light in the dark.

Keeping in step with the people who don't yet know Christ as we do, ready to share him when the time is right.

**John and Sue Ritter** have worked with young people for years and years and, yes, they understand them better than most old people (sorry, older people). They now sing and share their faith together as *Keep in Step*, and encourage young Christians and youth leaders to keep their witness lively and relevant to their culture.

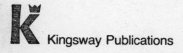

Kingsway Publications

# The Teenage Survival Kit

## by Pete Gilbert

*How can I be really committed to Jesus?*
*Does prayer have to be boring?*
*What's all this fuss about praise and worship?*
*What can a Christian do in a war-torn,*
 *money-grabbing world?*

If you want to be honest with God, take him seriously and set about living your life to please him, then this book has a lot to offer you.

Pete Gilbert knows that Christianity works. That an ongoing relationship with Jesus today can be a satisfying and fulfilling experience. In this book he spells out how you can find what thousands of others are discovering: a faith that makes a difference, a real alternative to the insecure, unstable and out-of-control existence that so many call twentieth-century living.

You can survive—you can enjoy *real* life to the full, if you'll accept the challenge Jesus makes today: 'Follow me.'

**Pete Gilbert** co-ordinates the work of British Youth for Christ in London.

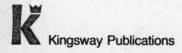

Kingsway Publications

# Sex and Young People

## by Lance Pierson

*Are Christians anti-sex?*

> *What has the Bible got to do with sex in the twentieth century?*

*How can I resist the pressure to conform when 'everybody's doing it'?*

> *How do I keep physical love special in a world that downgrades and cheapens sex?*

This book answers these questions—and many others—in a plain-speaking, straightforward way. It looks at the myths and lies that the world is out to sell—and the truth of God's word which puts things in perspective. It faces the problems and fears that trouble young people today.

No simple formula—no cold-hearted preaching—just honest answers to real questions.

**Lance Pierson** has been a teacher and Scripture Union worker. Thousands of young people have appreciated his honest, sympathetic approach to sexual problems and questions. He is married with two children.

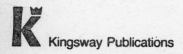

Kingsway Publications